In *Everything is Change* Beatrice Walditch shows how contemporary ideas of an ever-emergent cosmos are also part of the traditional worldview in places as far apart as Greece and China. This understanding of how the world works is in complete contrast to Christian concepts and the various successors – including supposedly secular science as well as modern paganism.

Seeing the world as ever-emergent provides a clearer understanding of divination and enchantment as they were practised in northern Europe before Christianity. It also stimulates new ways of thinking about modern day life, including how our self-identities are also in a continual state of renewal and creation.

*Everything is Change* is the fourth book in the Living in a Magical World series. These books will challenge you to recoergnise the traditional magic still alive in modern society, and empower you with a variety of skills and insights.

Previous books by Beatrice Walditch
from Heart of Albion

*You Don't Just Drink It!*
*What you need to know – and do – before drinking mead*

*Listening to the Stones*
(Volume One of the Living in a Magical World series)

*Knowing Your Guardians*
(Volume Two of the Living in a Magical World series)

*Learning From the Ancestors*
(Volume Three of the Living in a Magical World series)

Living in a Magical World:
Volume Four

# Everything is Change
## Beatrice Walditch

**Heart of Albion**

# Everything is Change

## Beatrice Walditch

ISBN 978-1-905646-28-9

© Text copyright Beatrice Walditch 2016

© illustrations copyright contributors 2016

*Front cover:* Swallowhead Springs near Silbury Hill, Wiltshire.

The moral rights of the author and illustrators have been asserted. All rights reserved. No part of this book may be reproduced in any form or by any means without prior written permission from Heart of Albion, except for brief passages quoted in reviews.

Published by

**Heart of Albion**
113 High Street, Avebury
Marlborough, SN8 1RF

albion@indigogroup.co.uk
Visit our Web site: www.hoap.co.uk

Printed in England by Booksprint

# Contents

| | |
|---|---|
| A state of emergency | 1 |
| Meet the Eenie-Weenie | 4 |
| Process all the way down | 7 |
| Keeping up the day | 8 |
| The carrying stream of memory | 10 |
| The emergence of sacred places | 11 |
| Rethinking animism | 13 |
| Rethinking reincarnation | 16 |
| Rethinking chaos | 18 |
| The web of *wyrd* | 20 |
| Charismatic and gifted | 20 |
| The power of the leech | 22 |
| The cauldron of creativity | 23 |
| The queens of the valleys | 27 |
| Destiny and divination | 29 |
| The divine *versus* diviners | 32 |
| The multiplicity of mantic arts | 33 |
| Portents and harbingers | 36 |
| Five helpful hints | 38 |
| The game of life | 39 |

| | |
|---|---|
| Life as a journey | 40 |
| The myths of pilgrimage | 42 |
| Walking in the here and now | 44 |
| The way and the waymarks | 45 |
| Life as a wayfarer | 47 |
| The *wyrmas* breath | 47 |
| The babbling and bubbling meditation | 52 |
| The ever-changing changeless tradition | 53 |
| Ever-changing deities | 56 |
| The Orders or Choirs of Christian angels | 58 |
| Emergent self-identity | 59 |
| Identity fluidity | 60 |
| Personae are more than pseudonyms | 63 |
| Investing in amulets | 65 |
| Alternatives to amulets | 67 |
| Playtime for personae | 69 |
| Creating personae | 70 |
| Visualisation, ritualisation and actualisation | 71 |
| That's why it's magic | 72 |
| Acknowledgements | 73 |
| Sources | 74 |

for Poppy Palin – fellow walker in the wild

*The salmon of knowledge. Illustration by Ian Brown.*

# A state of emergency

> I am a wind on the sea,
> I am a wave of the ocean,
> I am the roar of the sea,
> I am a bull of seven battles,
> I am a hawk on the cliff,
> I am a teardrop of sunlight,
> I am a gentle herb,
> I am a boar enraged,
> I am a salmon in a pool,
> I am a lake in a plain,
> I am the vigour of man
> I am the meaning of poetry,
> I am a spear on the attack, pouring forth combat,
> I am the god who fires your mind.

This are the words of Amergin Glúingel as he first set foot on Ireland, as recorded in the eleventh century *Lebor Gabála Érenn* or *Book of Invasions* and translated by Lloyd D. Graham.

What strikes me most is that, on the basis of this account, Amergin is exceptionally active, even by the standards of self-proclaimed gods. Almost all the lines refer to doing something, or to being something which is alive. Even the 'meaning of poetry' is ever-evolving as each time a poem is uttered the listeners will form different understandings. And if you think this is stretching metaphors just a bit too far then the rest of this book should make it clear then, far from me stretching ideas too far, you are simply not accustomed to stretching your assumptions very far at all!

Amergin was not the only ancient Irish deity-like being to have such thoughts. As the Old Woman of Beare reputedly said:

> … What was flow
> is now all ebb. Ebbing I go.
> After the tide, the undertow.

This is a poem known as *An Cailleach Bhéara*, or *The Lament of the Old Woman of Beare*, which appeared in full in the previous book in this series.

There is a more concise version of this notion, written at least a thousand years previously by the Greek-speaking Heraclitus: *panta rhea*, usually translated as 'everything flows'. If you've ever said something like 'You can't step into the same river twice' then you've misquoted Heraclitus.

At the same time as Heraclitus was composing pithy epithets at Ephesus on the coast of the eastern Mediterranean, Lao Tsu was composing terse sentiments in southern China. The *Tao te Ching* (also known as the *Daojiao* or *Laozi*) uses the flow of water as the main metaphor for the nature of reality.

While the idea of an individual 'going with the flow' is more of a Western misunderstanding of Daoism, the notion of the whole of creation 'going with the flow' is more authentically Oriental. Lao Tsu describes Dao using water-related images such as 'the valley of the world', a 'deep pool' and 'at the bottom of everything'.

Spontaneity (*wuwei*) and transformation (*shengsheng buxi*) are key to understanding the Daoist view of the world. More accurately, these Chinese words translate as 'uncontrived action' and 'ceaseless generativity'. They carry no baggage of inherent or implied moral assumptions, so fly in the face of stodgy Confucianism conservatism – and its close cousin, the neo-Platonic Idealism of the medieval church and post-Reformation successors. In Daoism birth and change are the only 'rules'. As indeed they are for anything which is alive.

From a slightly different viewpoint, change is the essence of existence. Think about it. Anything which is alive is always changing. Even rocks and inanimate objects weather and degrade, albeit over much longer timescales than any living creature. As all astrophysicists observe, change is the only constant in the universe.

The only constant is change itself – 'the ever-changing changeless'. The cosmos exists to create and transform – and does so in abundance. Not for nothing is the *I Ching* or *Yijing* known in English as the *Classic of Changes*. Divination is, after all, the art of predicting changes – or understanding the processes behind the changes.

The musician Björk, on her album *Homogenic* – which I take to mean 'self-creating' – describes life as a 'state of emergency'. This neatly

*The upper reaches of the Wiltshire Avon. This water will flow through the Neolithic henge at Marden and then close to Stonehenge before flowing through a part of Hampshire with numerous prehistoric sites and then into the Solent.*

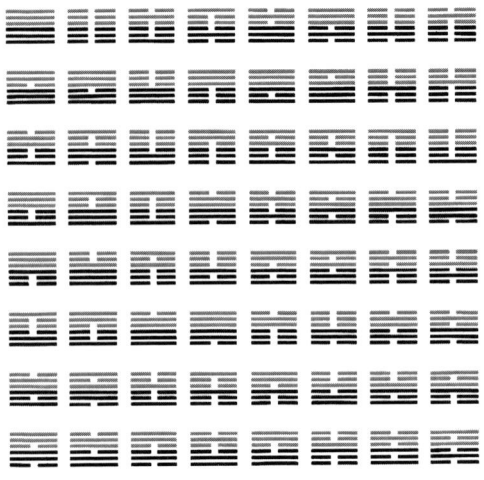

*The sixty-four heagrams of the Yijing or Book of Changes.*

blends emergence with excitement, exactly the same ideas which will be explored in this book.

If all this seems a little obscure then remember the words of the nursery rhyme:

> Row, row, row your boat, gently down the stream,
> Merrily, merrily, merrily, life is but a dream.

# Meet the Eenie-Weenie

Thinking of the universe as spontaneously emergent is fundamentally different from Western notions of evolution. These is no underlying cause-and-effect, still less a notion of 'triumphalism' to something better. An emergent cosmos is simply a playful one, creating new ways of being simply because it knows no other. The universe is alive in the same way that any living creature is alive, not specifically in the way that we think of human-like beings as being alive. Nothing just 'is', everything is 'doing' – just as Amergin put into poetry.

Western worldviews seldom stop to question the assumption that the universe runs according to 'cause and effect' and so can be reduced to 'reason'. But this seemingly secular assumption is, in reality, the unchallenged assumption that there is a God in charge of everything. Take away the deity who causes this, has that effect, acts reasonably and any number of other theological presumptions and the whole

Above: 'Tantric Twisted Rope.' A wall hanging by the Japanese textile artist Serizawa. Similar interlace motifs are part of medieval Scandinavian and Anglo-Saxon art. Should we think of these as 'Eeenie-Weenies?

Right: Are the Eenie-Weenies also at play in this tenth century cross shaft from Llanfrynach?

edifice collapses. Just as the nature of a piece of wood is immanent in its shape and grain so too the nature of the world is immanent, not imposed by a transcendent deity.

Most people living in the West are desperate for this edifice of 'cause and effect' and externally-imposed 'ideals' not to collapse. Whether they identify as religious or secular, the thought that things can be otherwise is so unsettling as to be all-but unthinkable. The idea that the cosmos could be playful is anathema to both God-given creation and secular rationalism. In contrast, the philosopher – in the true sense of 'a lover of wisdom' – Alan Watts wrote back in 1962:

> Life seems to resolve itself down to a tiny germ or nipple of sensitivity. I call it the Eenie-Weenie – a sqiggling little nucleus that is trying to make love to itself and never can quite get there. The whole fabulous complexity of vegetable and animal life, as of human civilization, is just a colossal elaboration of the Eenie-Weenie trying to make the Eenie-Weenie.
>
> Alan Watts *The Joyous Cosmology*

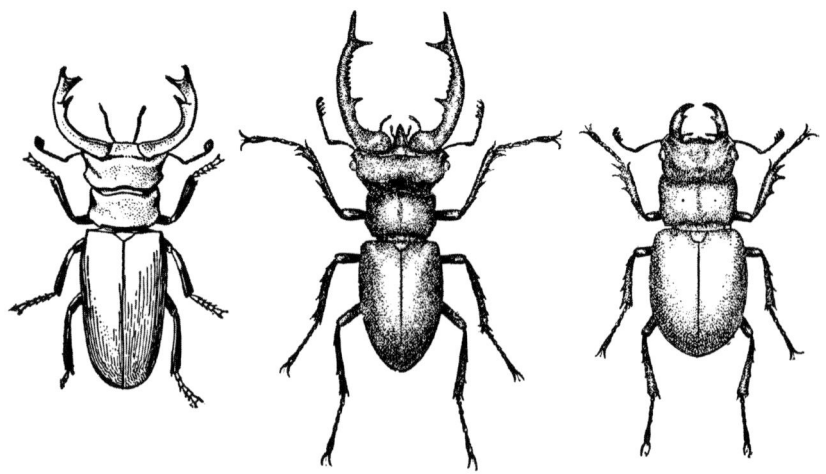

*Three of the many species of Stag Beetles (not to scale).*

Reality is made up of any number of ever-mutating 'Eenie-Weenies'. Zoologists have yet to determine how many types of beetles there are in the world – there seems to be a limitless variety, each of which are slowly but inexorably diversifying into subspecies and, eventually, new species.

The entirety of the universe is just a bigger version of the of beetle scenario, with as many 'species' and 'varieties' as human consciousness chooses to comprehend, each of which is capable of mutating. But human thinking is different in a crucial respect – ideas can evolve and mutate at the speed of thought and culture, and are not slowed down by cycles of reproduction. The number and complexity of possible 'realities' is limited only by the preconceptions and limited imagination.

'Reality' is not something which is out there to be discovered. Rather, it is something which is constantly emerging from human thinking. Some aspects of reality are tangible – but what makes humans most distinct from other animals is that our societies are not the sum total of material culture. Instead, our *immaterial culture* – the meaning and significance we give to the manifest world through 'knowledge', stories, songs and such like – is the more significant part of our realities. Indeed, there is no such thing as reality – only an ever-expanding number of realities. As Robert Anton Wilson once wrote, '"Reality" is some kind of ontological silly-putty.'

# Process all the way down

If cause-and-effect is not 'running the show' then what is? Clearly all realities are a response to changes. Human realities – otherwise known as cultures and societies – are the 'negotiated' responses to any manner of changes. Those 'negotiations' may be overt, whether confrontational or conciliatory, or they may be embedded deep within established norms of behaviour. Whichever, they involve some sort of communication, even if it is non-verbal. The overall term might be 'performed'.

So 'cultures' – or however you prefer to refer to the processes, events and relationships which make up 'societies' – are not fixed entities. Rather, they are performed and negotiated in response to changes. Contrary to views of some academics, this does not require a magical ingredient called 'agency' – peoples' interactions with their environment *are* everything.

This 'performance' can been termed 'dependent co-arising'. This is often expressed in the form of a parable. Before a table can exist there needs to be both wood and a carpenter. The tree which supplied the wood needed sunshine, rain and all the other ingredients of its environment. The carpenter needed to have learnt all the necessary skills. He too needs water and food, which are most probably supplied by people who are part of his wider society. Both the tree and the carpenter only came into existence because of countless generations of forebears. A billion years of evolution have come together to bring us the tree, the carpenter and thence the table. Even if you have never seen the table or the met the carpenter, your life is probably in some way linked to them. Most certainly your life too is the pinnacle of

*The classic illusion of a white vase that can also be seen as two faces in profile.*

unimaginably complex processes which go back to long before the human species.

Unlike the Greeks, Jews, Christians, pre-conversion Scandinavians and a whole host of traditional cultures, that Chinese worldview has no ultimate beginning or end. There are neither creation myths nor 'end time' myths. The nearest is the terse remark in the *Tao de Ching* that

> Dao gave birth to One
> One gave birth to Two
> Two gave birth to Three
> and Three gave birth to the multitude of things.

Unlike traditional cultures which envisage the world being supported by an elephant standing on a turtle, which in turn is supported by a countless succession of elephants and turtles, the Chinese worldview is 'process all the way down'. Every process we are consciously aware of is, so to speak, a fractal of one or more meta-processes. Dao is the all-pervasive process, both at the 'beginning' and throughout all later creation.

# Keeping up the day

Western culture is the sum total of these processes weaving together. We simply don't normally look at our own society in this manner. If we do, it is usually when looking nostalgically at 'olde worlde' customs. Commonly, traditional cultures are thought of rather like 'fossils' from the past, always on the brink of dying off. This is as true for our own traditions as it is for anthropological reports of seemingly-exotic Third World cultures.

For example, a hundred years ago there was a belief that English 'country dancing' was dying out and needed to be revived by earnest folklorists. The people who they 'collected' the dances from did not call it 'country dancing' – it was just what they did on high days and holidays. It was dying out – simply because new fashions were taking over, which the folklorists regarded with open contempt.

Morris dancing was just one of the types of dance which were collected, although has come to epitomise rural English culture, at least as viewed through the seriously distorting rose-tinted spectacles of nostalgia and 'heritage'. Morris dancing – and allied styles, such as molly dancing – have stayed alive. But they have done so largely by

*Medieval illustration of masked dancers.*

adapting to changing circumstances – not least the who, where, when and why of performances.

A better example of a folk custom would be stag nights and hen nights. Not least because one going to such an event thinks of them as folk customs! Each one is different to any other, and yet various activities are shared. Not just the drinking, but also the risqué behaviour and the all-important 'bonding' which makes the evening memorable, and the subject of anecdotal remarks whenever the participants meet up in the future. Yet the continuity does not inhibit innovation – indeed each such celebration is expected to add some new variation.

*Members of the Pig Dyke molly dancing team at Whittlesey Straw Bear Festival in January 2009.*

This is the 'process of reality' seen almost in microcosm. There is both spontaneity and a sense of following expectations of the 'done thing'. Similar remarks could be made about birthday parties. In counties which have annual rites to honour the ancestors – as outlined in *Learning from the Ancestors* – then these too follow customary practice without requiring a formal hierarchy of organisation. Countless other seasonal customs used to follow this pattern.

In some parts of the country helping to organise or just taking part in these annual events would have been termed 'keeping up the day'. Such activities were, if seen from the viewpoint of folklorists, always dying out. Looked at from the opposite end of the telescope, they are always innovating. So, while pioneering folklorists want to 'fossilise' customs and pickle them in aspic, the customs themselves wanted to stay alive by ever-mutating. Some did, some didn't. Revived customs too survive by mutating.

# The carrying stream of memory

If traditional cultures did not think of themselves in the same way as folklorists described them, then how did they think? One answer has been provided very clearly by Stanley Robertson (1940–2009) who is considered to be one of the most notable 'tradition bearers' within the Scottish Traveller community. He learnt a wealth of stories and songs from his great-aunt, Maggie Stewart, and other older members of the family while a child and sitting around camp fires as they moved around Aberdeenshire and further afield.

Although Stanley was to write a number of books, he learnt this lore purely by listening to the elders. His own renditions were done from memory. This process of transmission had of course continued over many centuries. Indeed, while the stories and songs themselves must have mutated beyond recognition, by definition this passing on from the old to the young goes back to the origins of language among primates.

Stanley referred to this way of on passing the lore of his people as 'the carrying stream of memory'. I, for one, can think of no better metaphor. That it also echoes the thinking of Heraclitus and Lao Tsu from two-and-a-half millennia ago only adds to its resonance.

*Looking east in the early morning along the River Kennet. This photograph was taken close to West Kennett chamber tomb. In the Neolithic the fields visible either side of the river had massive timber palisades where ritual pig feasts took place. Those occasions were most probably an opportunity to retell myths, legends and other stories.*

# The emergence of sacred places

So far my examples of deep-rooted processes have involved carpenters and storytellers. But the same processes are at work in the places which people inhabit. Where we live – whether city centre, suburb or village – is the sum total of everything that people have been doing there for generations. Even neat and tidy rows of nineteenth century housing which are so typical of British towns and cities are laid out according to the boundaries of fields which were once there before, because each 'developer' bought one or more fields. Those fields were, in all probability, laid out in the eighteenth century – but reflected earlier ways of dividing the land which seem to have come about around the tenth century. And so the layers of the onion keep peeling away...

We tend to think of the term 'sacred places' as something of a label which can be pinned on churches, temples, mosques, synagogues and such like – not least prehistoric stone circles such as Avebury, Castlerigg, Rollright and Stonehenge. Yet the reality is that such places are sacred less because of being labelled such, but because of the rituals which take place there. Only if 'sacred activities' are sustained – by 'the keeping up of the day' or more formal rites – do we think of a place as actually being sacred.

There are no hard and fast rules about what makes churches, henges or other places 'sacred'. Such a designation depends on ever-shifting cultural relationships between people and their environment. Above

*The Rollright Stones.*

*Waterfalls in the Grampians.*

all, these relationships are ongoing. In a sense a 'sacred place' is always emergent, never culturally static. If you like, a sacred place is to space as candle light is to a candle, or as a waterfall is to water. We can put a candle or a bucket of water in a museum, but no one can curate a flame or a whirlpool. Places can be 'conserved' but they are only 'sacred places' in so much as sacred rituals – however minimalistic – are performed there.

# Rethinking animism

If, as I am suggesting, the entire cosmos is continually in the process of creating and recreating itself, does that mean it is alive? Long ago anthropologists invented the term 'animism' to describe so-called 'primitive cultures' which believed that inanimate and inert objects – such as rocks – were imbued with life or spirit. Western concepts of discarnate souls were conflated with such 'spirits' leading to all manner of muddled thinking.

But clarity was never sought as such worldviews were deemed 'superstitions' – a term usually used derogatorily to refer to ways of thinking which conflicted with Christian beliefs. They were primitive

*Japanese rocks with* kami *are festooned with sacred ropes.*

and child-like, not the sort of beliefs which Colonial era grown ups considered commendable.

There was an even greater misunderstanding as these pioneer anthropologists failed to distinguish between spirits and deities which inhabited the likes of rivers, thunder, springs, sacred rocks and such like from the objects themselves. This total muddle lurks behind the term 'animism'. In reality, the people who best conform to this invented notion of animism are Westerners who believe that there are beings living on distant planets with cognitive skills comparable to humans.

Once anthropologists began to study traditional societies in a sympathetic manner they discovered that there is no one way of being 'animist'. Instead there any many 'ways of being' as part of a world continually being formed and reformed. Just as the weather continually changes as the oceans and the earth interact with the sky, so societies continually shift and change as the various aspects of the human realm interact with each other and the natural world. And this 'weather world' metaphor applies as much to modern Western society as to the most remote traditional peoples.

What confuses Westerners is that this is not the narrative we normally identify with. We are so accustomed to understanding the theory of something but doing something different that we scarcely notice when we construct one narrative but live according to another. When we

*The sun setting behind the Cove at Avebury.*

refer – as almost all English-speakers do – to the sun rising and the sun setting we all know that this is not strictly true as the sun never sets. Instead where we are on the planet is rotating, quite rapidly, with respect to the sun's position. But 'sunrise' and 'sunset' are much easier to get our heads – and tongues – around. Similarly most people betting on the lottery each week understand enough about the odds to realise they are more likely to be struck by lightning than win the jackpot. But millions of people reject this logical 'narrative' in favour of one that envisages them lifted out of their current financial circumstances.

What has this to do with whether we think the universe is alive or not? Well alive or dead are both 'merely' narratives. The better term might be 'myths', in that myths can be considered as narrative accounts of ideologies. You could believe one myth but still live your life according to a different narrative. I live as an animist – in the sense used by the current generation of anthropologists. I do not however feel a need to create a myth of a weather-like world being a cognitive being. You may have different needs. That does not mean we do not live in the same world...

# Rethinking reincarnation

> A second time was I formed.
> I have been a blue salmon.
> I have been a dog; I have been a stag;
> I have been a roebuck on the mountain.
> I have been a stock, I have been a spade
> I have been an axe in the hand;
> I have been a pin in a forceps,
> A year and a half;
> I have been a speckled white cock
> Upon hens in Eiddyn.
> I have been a stallion over a stud.
> I have been a violent bull,
> I have been a buck of yellow hue…

These are the words of Taliesin, as translated from medieval Irish by Lloyd Graham. There is a similar section in *The Battle of the Trees*. Again this is Graham's translation:

> I have been a tear in the air,
> I have been the dullest of stars.
> I have been a word among letters,
> I have been a book in the origin.
> I have been the light of lanterns,
> A year and a half.
> I have been a continuing bridge,
> Over three score Abers. [river mouths]
> I have been a course, I have been an eagle.
> I have been a coracle in the seas:
> I have been compliant in the banquet.
> I have been a drop in a shower;
> I have been a sword in the grasp of the hand
> I have been a shield in battle.
> I have been a string in a harp,
> Disguised for nine years.
> in water, in foam.
> I have been sponge in the fire,
> I have been wood in the covert.

These are lists of reincarnations. But not reincarnations as we normally think of them. Indeed literary scholars prefer such terms as 'metamorphoses'. But why shouldn't we take these poems as evidence of early Irish concepts of reincarnation?

One of the few things the Romans more-or-less reliably tell us about the Iron Age priest of Gaul and the British Isles – 'Druids' if you must – is that they believed in reincarnation. But these sources do not say that these priests believed in reincarnation in the same way as people about two thousand years later believed in reincarnation. There is no evidence that back then the idea of reincarnation involved souls – discarnate versions of our self-identities – being hosted by a succession of bodies. Such a worldview requires a dualism between body and mind which only developed during the last thousand years, mostly as part of the Protestant phase of Christianity, although it evolved into the dominant assumption of secularised modern Western societies.

What the medieval Irish sources seem to be telling us is exactly what the hippies of the late 1960s discovered: 'We are stardust'. That is, the atoms which make up our bodies have already been 'recycled' squillions of times in all manner of disparate entities, some animate, many not. Taliesin could never have understood atoms in the way we do. But he expressed the same understanding far more poetically than any modern physicist.

What is significant about this conception of reincarnation is that without death and rebirth there is no change. Birth and death are not so much a dualism as two 'phases' of the same process. We are what we are in large part because of our parents and antecedents, and pass that legacy – whether good, bad or indifferent – on to our children.

Furthermore, Taliesin almost certainly was the reincarnation of a 'Druid' encountered by Romans, in that the same view of reincarnation was presumably shared over the centuries. This ever-emergent way of 'recycling' our material beings makes so much more sense than Christian notions of discarnate 'consciousness' popping back into different bodies. At least it makes more sense from within the ever-emergent cosmos which this book explores.

# Rethinking chaos

Reading the Classical Greek myths we encounter the same emergent worldview. Everything comes from Chaos, the primeval void or 'yawning gap'. Modern usage of the word 'chaos' infers that this was 'chaotic'. Seemingly it was thought of by the Greeks as a shapeless mass – that's certainly how the Roman poet Ovid regarded it.

But take away the sense of chaotic – a word only invented in the eighteenth century – and the Greek Chaos becomes another example of an ever-emergent cosmos. This is chaos as creative – forming the hitherto unformed, as any painter, sculptor, poet, writer, composer and other 'creative person' does. If the cosmos is self-creating from this 'chaos' perhaps it is less a universe – literally 'all things turned into one' – than a Chaosmos.

Emergence is not chaotic or even random. Instead everything is created according to the forms of nature – a concept indistinguishable from earlier notions of divine order. The branches of trees, the watercourses in estuaries and the microscopic crystals of metals all form similar dendritic shapes. Clouds can take on the appearance of sand dunes, the markings on mackerel, horses' tails, anvils, faces, and an array of other simulacra. Everything which is emergent is, in principle, predictable. In practice we usually struggle to see the as-yet

*Many plants confirm to the Fibonacci series.*

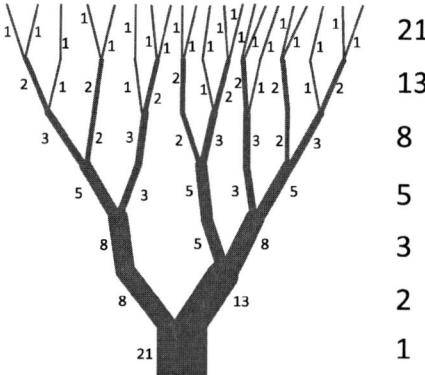

unfulfilled pattern, despite making prophetic presumptions based on probabilities, prophesies or portents.

Nietzsche anticipated all this when he wrote 'One must have chaos in oneself to give birth to a dancing star.'

In the 1960s a meteorologist, Edward Lorenz, was studying the unpredictability of air currents. His mathematical modelling established that small changes in the measured conditions now could lead to dramatically different future outcomes. In his own words '... the present determines the future, but the approximate present does not approximately determine the future.' His 'models', when plotted out, looked rather like the wings of butterflies. This in turn led to the over-stated analogy that a butterfly flapping its wings in Brazil just might cause a tornado in Texas – the so-called 'butterfly effect'.

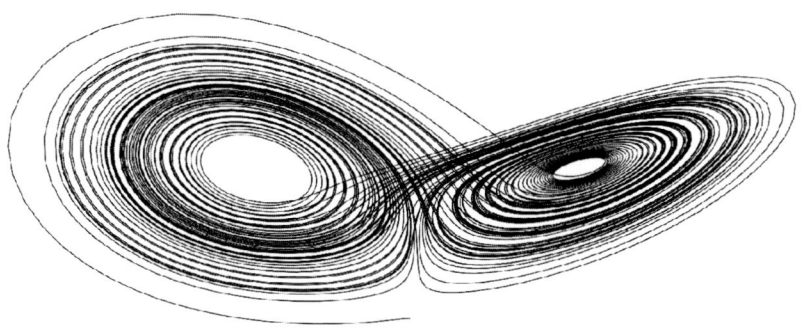

*Lorenz attractor plot.*

Other researchers recognised that these mathematical models of 'unstable' systems accurately depict other complex processes, as diverse as traffic congestion and financial markets. The whole approach was termed 'Chaos Theory'. To the mathematicians involved the word chaos has a slightly different meaning than in everyday language – although that distinction was lost on any number of popular authors who popularised these ideas.

Why I am trying to rethink and clarify Chaos? Because, by taking away the confusion with chaotic, both the ancient Greeks and modern mathematicians have a concept of chaos which is entirely in accord with an ever-emergent cosmos. This is the sense of the 'Chaosmos' I want to carry forward into the rest of this book.

# The web of *wyrd*

In Scandinavian sagas the concept of *wyrd* conveys something of the weaving of everything that makes up the world. This is fairly typically of many traditional cultures as weaving is often seen as a simile for the cosmos itself. In many of these societies spinning and weaving is predominately done by women and girls, so there is a further association with the 'generative' aspect of creation. And, equally commonly, there is a belief that spells can be woven into the cloth – usually as protection for the menfolk or other family members who will be wearing the finished clothes.

In my own experience even the simple act of plaiting three strands together to make a simple strap almost automatically brings to mind 'weaving' in either a blessing or protective 'curse' in the name of three deities (see *Knowing Your Guardians* in this series). Any number of traditional weaving patterns use 'endless' motifs aimed at trapping the attention of the Evil Eye or otherwise averting witchcraft.

# Charismatic and gifted

There is another concept which is all-but ubiquitous in traditional cultures yet, curiously , there is no word in modern English. The Polynesian word *mana* is commonly used, but even this is confusing as it has become understood as 'the stuff of magic' or some unspecified 'life force' that permeates the universe. These misunderstandings largely reflect the difficulty that Western minds have with what *mana*

Top: *Drawing of a Yekuana basket. This pattern represents a poisonous snake called Awadi.*

Above: *A knitted Arran sweater. Traditionally the patterns offered protection and also helped identify the wearer.*

actually denotes. Those who have really studied what this word refers to report that it is a combination of charisma with a specific sense of the word 'gift' – as in a 'gifted child'.

This makes *mana* close kin to Japanese *kami* – 'specialness' of certain trees and rocks and also of powerful business leaders. The Japanese view is that *kami* is not generated by these trees, rocks or people but manifests most clearly through them. The source of *kami* is everywhere and nowhere – it is not a 'gift of the gods' as such.

With this understanding of *mana* and *kami* then a whole host of words in other languages also become clear. For examples, in pre-Islamic north Africa *baraka* denoted the sacredness of certain persons, healing plants and other physical objects. In sub-Saharan Africa the words include *ashe, bwanga* and *amanda* – often used to refer to the potency of medicines. In the New World there are numerous such words, such as *manitou* and *Wah'Kon*. In Tibetan it is referred to as *tse*, while in Indian languages the words *shakti* and *prakriti* have the primary sense of such charisma-cum-gift (although also refer to its manifestations). As far away as Australia there is *boolya*, *koochie* and *arangquiltha*. In Finnish the word is *väki* – a property thought to manifest in the steam from saunas.

The Sarawak people of Borneo have been influenced by Christian missionaries but still use their traditional word *lalud* to refer to the 'power of Christ', especially in contexts associated with healing. *Lalud* is thought of as a liquid, akin to blood permeating the whole of creation. Crystals and thunderstorms alike are 'powerhouses' of *lalud*.

Within European Christianity a saint's wonderworking power was known in Latin as *virtus* or *vim*. The latter had the specific sense of potency. Indeed the earlier Latin word for the power of Christ manifesting through a (living) priest or (dead) saint was *potentia* – the root of the modern words 'potent' and 'potency'. This *potentia* seemingly merges with ideas of the 'breath of life' to becomes the rather fizzy concept of the *Sanctus Spiritus*, or 'Holy Ghost', which makes up the third aspect of the Holy Trinity. In contrast to pre-conversion views, *potentia* had a very specific source – it was the power of Christ.

# The power of the leech

*Potentia* and *virtus* are effectively killed off by the Reformation. But if we look back at the origins of the same ideas then two words are used in pre-conversion Scandinavia to describe something which is very similar. One is *ond* and the other is *óðr* (pronounced '**oo**-ther'). One way of understanding the name of the deity *Oðinn* is to think of him as having *óðr* 'in him' – in other words, being full of *óðr*. Similarly in Old English there are also several words. One is *wod* – which arguably makes Wodin the deity full of *wod* – in other words *wod* manifests through him. The other word is *leac* (pronounced like 'leek' or 'luck') which has the primary sense of potency.

*Leac* is the direct ancestor of the name for the vegetable with a potent smell (and, at least in the wild varieties, a rather 'potent' shape) and the byname 'leech' for a doctor. Nothing to do with blood-sucking parasites but everything to do with the *leechdom-* – the knowledge (think wis(e)-dom) of which medicinal plants and charms were most powerful. An Anglo-Saxon *leech* would have cut these healing herbs (or 'wort's) with a *leac seax* – a 'knife of power'.

A leac seax.

Something of this sense of *leac* can be found in the little-used East Anglian word spirament. This has the sense of 'luck' – as in a 'lucky horseshoe' – and the 'stuff of life and magic'.

Although words such as *leac, óðr, potentia, mana* and *kami* have overlapping meanings we must be careful not to render them into some homogenous mental 'soup'. There is scope for several distinct words to be current at the same time. The clearest example is in Chinese where words such as *qi, de* and *jing* (also Romanised as *ch'i, te* and *ching*) have evolving and overlapping meanings. Chinese *qi* influences Japanese thinking – for example it is the '-ki' of Reiki.

Western languages and worldviews are seemingly unique in not having a word for a pervasive 'charisma-cum-gift'. This is presumably because, in complete contrast to older thinking, after the conversion to Christianity such a 'gift' was considered to come only from Christ and merged into ideas about the Sanctus Spiritus or Holy Ghost. However once the original sense of words such as *leac* and *óðr* are recognised then there is little difficulty in fitting this all-pervasive 'spirit' into an ever-emergent cosmos. Care is needed, however, not to reduce the concept to some vague 'life force' or 'stuff of magic'. Instead think of potency, charisma and the specific sense of 'gift'.

## The cauldron of creativity

In Welsh mythology this 'charismatic gift' is *awen* (pronounced 'á-wen' not 'ar-wen'). There are various ways of thinking about *awen*. For example, the leader of a modern Druid order, Greywolf, regards *awen* as 'the flowing spirit'. But at the core of the various interpretation is the sense of continual creativity.

According to a twelfth century poem in Welsh by Llywarch ap Llywelyn 'The Lord God will give me the sweet Awen, as from the

*The Cauldron of Rebirth. Illustration by Ian Brown.*

cauldron of Ceridwen.' The legends of Ceridwen tending a cauldron of inspiration seem to go back to at least the ninth century. For a year and a day she brews up a cauldron of *awen* (often translated into English as 'inspiration'). By accident a young boy, Gwion Bach, tastes three drops and transforms into the poet Taliesin.

*Rosmerta and her churn.*

During the Roman era in Gaul an all-providing goddess called Rosmerta was depicted with a churn. In societies where wealth was measured not by expensive cars but by cattle, then butter had a status which greatly exceeds modern day notions. Churns and cauldrons may function differently but are difficult to distinguish iconographically. We can reasonably assume that Ceridwen had her counterparts in other north European cultures.

*A replica Neolithic pot. Did prehistoric people also think that such cauldron-shaped vessels seethed with endless creativity?*

Left: *The Gundestrup cauldron, probably made between 200 BCE and 300 CE.*
Right: *Drawing of the panel which might depict the myth of cauldrons miraculously restoring life.*

Cauldrons by their very nature simmer for a long time, emitting steam all the while and often bubbling away too. The individual ingredients become difficult to recognise and the resulting brew is akin to the 'primordial soup' of Chinese creation myths. This is often compared to *wanton* soup – the Asian counterpart to minestrone but with fluffy 'dumplings' called *wanton* floating on the top. These dumplings are thought to resemble clouds floating over the primordial ocean.

As Robert Cochrane was moved to observe:

> The cauldron is... constantly moving, creating, bringing forth, tearing down, building up movement – one thing becomes the other, as also life becomes death and death life.' '... the simplest way of expressing what the cauldron is not is by saying 'be still'.
>
> (Cochrane 2002: 34)

On another occasion Cochrane wrote "The cauldron... means movement, a becoming of life - ever giving birth, ever creating new inspiration. There is within the cauldron all things and all future – fate.' (Cochrane 2002: 27) This was because the cauldon is where past, present and future are still in a state of flux and promise. Individual strands of 'fate' can be drawn out from this ever-changing 'potential' until the time comes for them to be cut and gathered up again in the mix, to be reformed in a new guise. It was the place of rebirth – at least according to the view of reincarnation in the previous section.

This metaphor of an ever-creating cauldron is central to my own thoughts about how *awen* – or *leac* or *óðr* or whatever – are continually arising. There are inevitably other ways of thinking about where and how this 'charismatic gift of creativity' arises but the steadily simmering cauldron, emitting reincarnation *väki*-like vapours does it for me.

## The queens of the valleys

There is nothing remarkable about 'cosmic' cauldrons and churns being associated with women. After all this simply reflects real life. But there is more to this than women's domestic roles. Equally obviously, women are most obviously the source of life and early nourishment. And that in turn goes deeper. Women are the bearers of something which is even more culturally significant in many, if not all, traditional societies: the ancestral blood line.

Until recent decades and the advent of DNA testing then paternity could at best only be assumed. Throughout the world it is the female line which determines identity. Famously, one is Jewish only if one's mother is Jewish. Less well-known is that the same basis for ethnicity is traditional among New World tribes such as the Hopi.

Irish myths repeatedly tell how a king could only inaugurated if he symbolically married the female sovereign-goddess of the land. His eligibility to be king came from his mother's blood line, even if he was regarded as the son of a powerful leader. The idea that the queen's blood line is all-important persists into medieval and modern myths about descendants of the Virgin Mary. The notions of a British 'royal family' – largely invented in the 1920s – are an attempt to reinstate the perceived purity of monarchical genes. Excessive tabloid interest in the wives of the male heirs to the throne has, in my mind, its medieval counterpart in the accounts – by Christian converts – of Irish kings reputedly mating with mares then bathing in the broth made from the horse's flesh. If nothing else, they share the same tendencies to sensationalism.

Strip away the sensationalism and we see that sovereignty was granted when the goddess offered the prospective king *derflaith* – the 'red drink' also described as mead and the drink of inspiration. Such a potent brew would have been prepared in a cauldron. Ceridwen was concocting a close counterpart.

*Swallowhead Springs, near Silbury Hill.*

Careful study of a cluster of modern words suggests that there is a common origin to words such as queen, kin, kind, quim (and a commonly-used counterpart) along with words for wedge-shaped (cuni – as in 'cuneiform' – and canine) and the words canal and channel (presumably originally denoting watercourses which were rather V-shaped in section). This suggests that women were associated with the upper reaches of valleys – the sovereigns of the land.

The presence of these words in a wide variety of Indo-European languages provides an indication of when this idea of 'valley goddesses' was current. Certainly during the Iron Age and, in Britain, quite plausibly in the middle of the Bronze Age (around 1500 to 1000 BCE). The word 'king' fits in here too, but is much later. Which in turn reveals something about prehistoric societies, although it is difficult to be more specific.

In modern society we, quite rightly, bend over backwards not to associate women only with child-rearing and domestic chores. However that should not blind us to the deep-rooted myths seemingly going back thousands of years which have regarded women as the bearers of the all-important 'tribal' bloodline, sovereigns of the land, and the keepers of the cauldrons of 'inspiration'. Such mythic perspectives on female identity are entirely in accordance with a continually creative cosmos. Modern society may well wish to add additional female roles, but this should not be at the expense of forgetting the fundamental ones.

Modern Western sensibilities have diminished the respect shown to our elders and antecedents. But, as explored in the previous book in this series *Learning From the Ancestors*, we are all part of an unbroken 'blood line' of mothers and fathers.

# Destiny and divination

> Human experience only exists in the present moment. The past exists as memories re-experienced in the present. The future exists as expectations or fantasies, again created in the present.
>
> Peter J. Carroll

Horoscopes, Tarot readings and a host of other divinatory 'arts' are ostensibly about foretelling the future. But awareness – however tentative or incomplete – of the future influences how we respond to forthcoming events. At the most clichéd it means that any girl told by a fairground 'Gypsy Rose Lee' that she will marry a tall, dark and handsome stranger will respond differently to such encounters than she will to meetings with men she is already acquainted with, especially if they are average height and blond. We may not be

*The eight trigrams of the Yijing.*

Left: *The Wheel of Fortune card from the Rider-Waite tarot set.*
Right: *The designs on a Siberian shaman's drum. One of the divination rituals was to cast either beans, small pebbles or the knuckle bones of animal onto the drum. The shaman then divined the future according to how and where they fell .*

consciously aware of any changes in our behaviour after reading the formulaic horoscope in a magazine, but at the very least they will instil a confidence – or, perhaps, uncertainty – that we did not have before.

Those who have some experience of both divination and enchantment concur that there is a considerable overlap in the middle. Divination is also about *inducing* changes. Bear in mind that the *Yijing (I Ching)* is usually translated as the 'Classic of Changes'. Not because – as some Western interpreters have proposed, because the six lines can be 'changeable', thereby allowing more complex predictions – but because the *Yijing* is actually 'tapping into' the changes inherent in the cosmos. Bear in mind that Daoism has its origins during the late Shang dynasty (*circa* 1200 to 1050 BCE) in divinatory rites using oracle bones.

Contrary to popularist Western ideas, a Tarot reading does not divine the future – it helps creates it. All divination, from this perspective, could be thought of as a form of counselling. Both divination and counselling 'reprise' and 'revise' the significant of the past to allow the

*A medieval depiction of two astrologers*

desired future. The boundaries between divination and enchantment are blurry. Indeed divination is inherently slippery – it exists in the gap between belief and knowledge where the future is always emergent, never fully formed. Some people view the future through statistical probabilities and spreadsheets, others through astrological charts or spreads of cards. *Sub specie aeterniti,* any epistemological differences are hard to discern.

*Dowsing, whether with bent rods or a pendulum, is also known as 'water divining'. While modern sensibilities tend not to put bent coat hangers in the same mental category as Tarot cards or birth charts, they all allow us to see a little more clearly the creative and emergent processes of the cosmos.*

# The divine *versus* diviners

Divination sits between two complex human traits. One the one hand, few people are comfortable with the idea that their lives are not governed by complex processes of cause-and-effect. 'Blind Chance' and her modern physics equivalent, chaotic systems, may be really running the show, but human minds seek reasons and seemingly-logical connections, even when none exist. We need to impose order according to patterns that conform to cultural norms. Without such causal connections our thinking risks being paralysed by uncertainty.

On the other hand, formal religions decree that one or more deities 'call the shots'. In contrast to impeccable divine interventions, foretelling the future is a riskier process. In modern thinking the divine and diviners are rarely regarded as companions. Christianity's abhorrence of augurers – other than its recognised prophets – is far from anomalous. Once again, divination occupied the slippery gap between the need for 'certainty' – or at least clarity – and faith. The Romans had no such problem – both senses of the word 'divine' come from Latin *divinus,* meaning 'of a god'. In Rome an augur sought to determine gods' own will, while the priests 'bribed' the gods to act according to the will of humans. Substitute 'wile' for 'will' if you prefer...

*Fortuna as 'Blind Chance'.*

# The multiplicity of mantic arts

Contrary to all these previous remarks, in the past foretelling the future was not about horoscopes and Tarot readings. Indeed divination was not specifically about the future. As the Scandinavian sagas state, the role of the Norns was to see the past, divine the present and foretell the future. The need to see the past was, of course, greater in the days before extensive literary records. In the age of photography and video we think little of seeing the past. Technology has also reduced the need to divine the present and also influences how we anticipate the future.

Traditionally there were any number of portents and harbingers which could offer insights. As Seneca wrote, the difference between Greeks and Etruscans is that

> whereas we believe lightning to be released as the result of the collision of clouds, they believe that clouds collide to create lightning. Because they attribute everything to the deity they do not believe that events have meaning in that they occur, but instead that they occur because they must have a meaning.

European society has sided with Seneca ever since. In Shakespeare's *As You Like It* the Duke extols the joys of hunting in the Forest of Arden, where he

> Finds tongues in trees, books in the running brooks,
> Sermons in stones, and good in everything.
> His attendant lord, Amiens, replies:
> Happy is your Grace,
> That can translate the stubbornness of fortune
> Into so quiet and so sweet a style.

In Skakespeare's own day this interchange of view was treading on thin ice as English society was still in the throes of religious revisionism. 'Sermons in stones', the witches in Macbeth and the various ghosts, such as Hamlet's father were niot just 'added colour'. To people of time they were the continuation of blatantly Catholic worldviews. A few years after these plays were published King James would rewrite the 'rule books'. Literally, as his translation of the Bible into English became the definitive one for English Protestants, and also more specifically in a book setting out how Biblical proclamations

*Aegeus consulting the oracle, or* Pythia, *at Delphi.*

about witches, divination and so forth should be reflected in early seventeenth century laws and society more broadly.

What was King James' problem? In the Old Testament there are numerous references to divination by fire, air, water, thunder, lightning and meteors. Specific techniques of divination mentioned in the Bible include astrology, casting lots, hepatoscopy (the inspection of livers of sacrificed animals), necromancy (prophesy by calling up the dead, as used by the Witch of Endor), oneiromancy (divination from dreams), rhabdomancy (divination using a rod or wand) and well as teraphim (an obscure divination technique using images).

The suffix '–mancy' is from the Greek word *mantikos,* meaning 'prophetic, oracular', which comes from *mantis,* translated as 'prophet' but with the literal sense of 'one touched by divine madness'. The Latin counterpart was *oraculum,* from which 'oracle' derives. The ancient Greeks famously had female oracles at several main temples, the most famous being the Pythia of Delphi. Delphi was regarded as the 'navel' or *omphalos* of the world, an *axis mundi* where place and time all come together, the 'here' and 'now' of all creation. What better place to foretell how things would emerge that at the very place of their emergence?

Even more interestingly the deity which originally presided over the Delphic temple was Python, always represented in Greek sculpture and vase-paintings as a serpent. In a later section I will return to serpents and their kin.

*A rubbing of a medieval memorial brass depicting a corpse.*

Some high-ranking Romans consulted professional augurs on what seems like a daily basis, although more typically as part of the sacrificial rites on major feast days. In western Scotland the kings' courts included hereditary augers called *frith*. This was pronounced 'free' and is the origin of the surname Freer. They were seers or 'see-ers', as in 'seeing the future' – a literal translation of the Latin *videns*. Popular Scottish culture includes many people, most often women, who were or are regarded as having 'second sight' or being 'fay'.

Anglo-Saxon law codes repeatedly prohibit divination. However one form of necromancy – known in Old English as *licwigelunga* ('corpse divination') transforms into the cult of saints' remains. This originated as an unauthorised practice but as the clergy recognised that there was serious money to be made from offerings to the saints' shrines, the practice became a dominant part of later medieval popular piety, until abruptly suppressed in the 1530s as part of the Reformation.

# Portents and harbingers

The word 'augury' originally had the narrower meaning of interpreting the signs from birds. We have an echo of this in saying about magpies:

> One for sorrow,
> Two for joy,
> Three for a girl,
> Four for a boy,
> Five for silver,
> Six for gold,
> Seven for a secret,
> Never to be told

and numerous variants. The sound of a skein of geese migrating at dusk – perhaps low enough to be hidden behind trees – still sounds eerie and ominous. Anyone in Finland and adjoining parts of Russia would immediately think that this was the sound of recently-deceased human souls making their way to the afterlife, somewhere north beyond the north wind. Other northern hemisphere cultures simply hear it as the sound of imminent death, akin to the banshee's cry in Ireland. Banshee in Irish is *bean sí*, the 'fairy woman' of the barrows. The word *sí* is discussed in more detail in *Knowing Your Guardians*.

Birds are among a number of notable portents in my own experiences. Asking permission to enter the site of an Iron Age sacred grove to select a piece of wood for making a staff has been answered by the unexpected appearance of

a kestrel – the only time I have ever seen a raptor when visiting that area. Clouds – especially their reflections in water – can also act as important portents. Ripples on water can themselves be 'read'. If the water is inherently still – as at holy wells – then drop pins, small stones or coins. Traditionally three were deposited in quick succession, though not at once. Remember too when lighting incense that the patterns formed by the smoke are susceptible to subtle drafts, such as your own breathing.

If divination forms part of a ritual taking place where there is no natural source of water then take a 'chalice' – using the word to signify a wide variety of bowl-like vessels – and add dark-coloured liquid. Port or another deep red wine fits in with my inclinatations but inky water is fine too. At one time I had little sachets of sepia from squids which produced an especially intense inkiness. Create ripples by blowing on surface – try to ask the question mentally or out load at more or less the same time. Then 'skry' the reflections of a candle flame.

Birds, clouds, ripples, smoke, wax dropped into water, tealeaves at the bottom of a cup – the list can be extended almost endlessly. What is important is not simply subtle shifts in the state of matter. Divination is taking place when these changing states of matter influence your state of mind. Or is it the other way about – your state of mind, specifically the 'question' in your mind, influencing the state of matter? Both are equally true. For a moment or so your state of mind and the 'state of emergent matter' have become as one.

# Five helpful hints

Five unrelated remarks before I move on. Firstly, there is little, if any, difference between asking permission of the *land wights* to cut their plants, perform a ritual in their presence, and such like and divining for the answer to the same questions. In both cases you are looking for a portent. (See *Knowing Your Guardians* for more information about *land wights*.)

Secondly, when consulting any sort of 'oracle' remember you are doing so because you feel a need to 'tap into' something wiser than you. And, if the oracle knows the answer to your questions better than you do, then they probably also know what the right question is better than you too! Despite what might be at the forefront of your worries or uncertainties, do not presume you necessarily know what to ask. Simple divination techniques suffice for simple yes-no questions. When we need to make more open-ended enquiries then there is only one question to ask first: 'What do I need to know?'

Third, regard divination rituals as you would any other ritual – make sure there is a clearly defined time and space. 'Closing' the ritual temporally and space is key. For all than divination blurs distinctions you do not want that 'blurring' to persist once you have resumed more mundane activities.

Fourth, remember that the future is not 'out there'. Instead it is being created here and now. Divination techniques are techniques for becoming immersed in that flux. How to become a more active part of that 'flux' will be the topic of the next book in this series, *Enchantment is All About Us.*

Finally, one big thought. Think of divination as 'ways of knowing' the world which go back long before specific religious ideologies. Certainly long before the secular successor to the Protestant version of these – modern Western rationalism – claimed exclusive access to the 'right way to know'. The deep flaw in the scientific paradigm is the unscientific attitude to ways of knowing which differ from its own. Think of it as endemic epistemological bigotry.

# The game of life

Just as Tarot cards evolve out of ordinary fifteenth century playing cards and dice are an improved version of the knuckle bones used for casting lots so other games of skill and chance seem to have had divinatory – and perhaps divine – counterparts.

Checkerboards – as used for 'checkers' or draughts and chess as well as a great more lesser known games – seem to be linked to the pattern used to decorate images of divine beings from India all the way to medieval Ireland. Board games of the Tablut and Hnefatafl type are different again, in that the two sides are made up of different numbers

Above: *The opening positions of Hnefatafl* .
Right: *A similar game would almost certainly have been known to the illustrator of the late seventh century* Book of Durrow.

and types of pieces. At the start of the game the king is in the 'sacred centre', surrounded by his army while the opposing side are around the circumference. This is clearly derived from a formalised way of thinking how the world should be – a microcosm if you like.

A similar layout is used for Fox and Geese (with slight variants known around the world by many names. But presumably by the time these evolve the concept of the king at a sacred centre has ceased to be part of common thinking. The same process can be seen with the invention of Ludo in 1896, which reduces the more complex Indian game of Pachisi, known to have been played in the sixth century and popular with the Mughal emporers, to a 'race game' based on little more than chance.

We tend to think that the chance and skill of board games are somewhat removed from the ways of the real world. However when these games were invented there would have been much closer associations. Over the intervening centuries our concepts of an ideal society and the causality of events have shifted significantly, while the games have evolved only more superficially. Assumptions about 'chance' and order still underpin modern day life. But those assumptions now manifest as video games and the like, not as board games.

# Life as a journey

I want to change tack a little and think about how we think of our passage through life. All of us impose some sort of narrative on our lives. A great many people become trapped in that narrative. To be sure there are often pragmatic reasons why decisions and events in the past have a massive influence on our options for day-to-day activities. But, contrary to popular belief, the *reasons* why are not cast in any sort of concrete. The narrative of our past is a in large part one massive metaphor.

Some people think that life is like a river – something that one is part of but not capable of being influenced. The most common meta-metaphor is that life is a journey. Indeed several thousand years ago – and more recently for some traditional societies – life was literally a journey – and endless journey along which every aspect of life took place.

*The River Wye near Preston on Wye, Herefordshire.*

Nomadic lives are inherently different to those of farmers cultivating the same fields year after year, and even more distinct from the suburban existence of those who commute to jobs in factories or offices. Little imagination in needed to recognise that life 'on the road' is continually emergent in ways that sedentary living rarely is. Modern society tends to romanticise the 'Gypsy life' – although I have enough friends who were part of the traveller movement of the 1980s to know that the reality lacks any such romance.

Yet clearly travelling has a lure which outweighs the many hardships. I would suggest that this is not simply a need to encounter novel places and make or renew friendships. Unconsciously we are seeking to get closer to an 'emergent' way of being. The human mind has evolved to deal effectively with uncertainty, to adapt, and embrace social and environmental changes – to the extent that most people feel something is missing from their lives if circumstances start to get too settled.

# The myths of pilgrimage

Most people attempt to fulfil this craving with an annual holiday or a more extended 'gap year'. Even in the largely secular modern society, the boundaries between such vacations and a sense of pilgrimage are often blurred. At one extreme are visits to recognised sacred places or religious retreats – possibly, though nor necessarily, with the journey there being explicitly a pilgrimage.

Towards the other extreme are the cheap package tours which allow plenty of sun worshipping at an ever-powerful liminal location – the boundary between sea and land – along with creating a liminal time for more-or-less transgressive behaviour. Club 18-30 holidays, and their Saga counterparts, are ritualised to at least the same extent as a fortnight meditating in an Indian ashram.

Pilgrimage is a wonderful metaphor for life. The destinations are fixed in advance. But the 'getting there' is everything. Unlike most other journeys, a pilgrimage is not merely a journey from home to elsewhere, just a life is more than a person's dates of birth and death. Pilgrimage also aims to be more than tourism, at least the sort of tourism which Hakim Bey eloquently summarised:

*The archetypal image of a medieval pilgrim.*

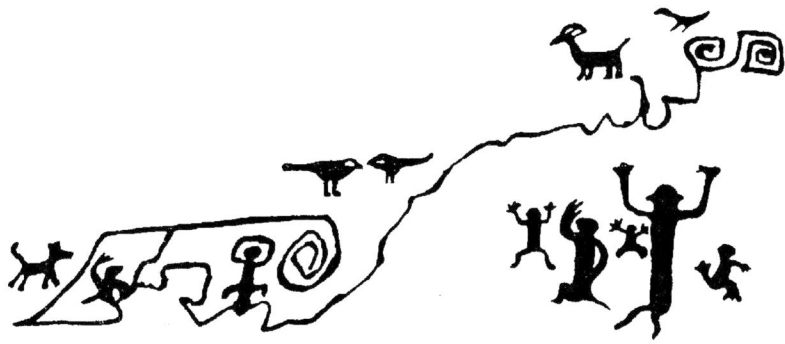

Even though tourists appear to be physically present in Nature or Culture, in effect one might call them ghosts haunting ruins, lacking all bodily presence. They're not really *there*, but rather move through a mind-scape, an abstraction ('Nature', 'Culture'), collecting images rather than experience. All too frequently their vacations are taken in the midst of other peoples' misery and even add to that misery.

(Bey no date [mid-1990s])

*In some respects Sir Galahad's quest for the Holy Grail is a European counterpart to Australian 'walkabouts' and their associated Dreamtime legends or Hopi mythicl journeys (as depicted at the top of the page).*

Pilgrimage is envisioned as more experiential, more immersive, more numinous. The reality is an ever-shifting mix along the spectrum. No pilgrimage is entirely 'in the moment' as the reason for the journey is to re-enact a sacred myth. This is as true for the walkabouts of Australian Aborigines as it is for Christians followed *El Camino*, or medieval routes to Canterbury. A journey lies at the core of the myths which identify a great many societies. The Israelites were led by Moses through the desert to their promised land. The Classical Greeks knew the legends of Odysseus and Jason. The life of Christ was peregrinatory. The Arthurian knights sought the Grail by numerous quests. Dante took a trip to Purgatory. His Protestant successor, John Bunyan, created an equally epic allegory of *Pilgrim's Progress*.

Even modern secular societies have wagon trails – either to the 'Wild West' or the Transvaal – as part of their mythologised identities. And after the colonial processes met up on the far side of the planet, space became the final frontier. Not for nothing was *Wagon Trek to the Stars* the provisional name for a TV scifi series.

# Walking in the here and now

What better than to simply regard all exploratory journeys as a manifestation of inherent emergence? The do not need to be grandified by notions of pilgrimage. Better that when walking along a route which is new to you, wherever the destination or whatever the purpose, you maintain a full sense of awareness of the here and now. Be alert to the novelty of everything. Should you walk this way again then your memory will dim that sense of discovery.

Whether walking on familiar paths or unfamiliar ones try to keep your stop your mind wandering onto topics which are not about what you can directly experience right now. As it were, limit your thought to the horizon. This is of course less restrictive walking on, say, open moors or downs than in a wood or somewhere more suburban.

Needless to say mobile phones and the like are totally taboo. While it is sensible to carry one in case of emergencies, there is no reason for it to be switched on. Even taking photographs is overly intrusive as we take them only for the sake of the future, often to share with 'absent friends'. As such they are not part of the here and now. In any event photographs can only capture a selective part of our experience, not the full extent of our vision, still less all the other senses.

This is something of the mindset of 'listening' to the landscape – with all our senses – which the first book in this series, Listening to the Stones was all about. I simply want to add to the suggestions in that book the observation that when we succeed in 'listening' to our surroundings in this fully-immersive manner then we have taken a key step towards being closer to the here and now, which is where the cosmos is continually emerging from. As such it is a way of experiencing which underpins the ability to divine the future and, as will be discussed in the next book, to 'enchant' the world. Since childhood walking has been the best way to 'get in touch' with the essence of existence.

# The way and the waymarks

No journey is homogenous. Even the most profound pilgrimage alternates between visits to shrines and stays in hostels. Every way has its waymarks as well as its wayfarers. Some ways are so famous as to have an abundance of shrines and an excessive of wayfarers. Other ways are those known to few apart from ourselves, where shrines are absent and companions rare. We need to create our own waymarks.

There is a two to three mile walk from my home which crosses over a packhorse bridge, then a modern wooden bridge spans a lesser watercourse. Soon after there is a stile through a hedge where the hawthorn and nettles intrude too readily. After that a pair of stiles span a linear wood. The path is through meadowland and the feet of walkers leave a clear wear path. A few hundred yards later the path leaves the valley bottom and heads up alongside a hedge. About halfway along are two mature ash trees, with complex roots. Further along are the scant remains of Bronze Age burial mounds, while more substantial ones stand as sentinels on the skyline. On the far side of the summit is the elder tree from which I cut the staff I use on such walks.

*The start of the route described.*

Suffice to say that each of these waymarks is significant to me, albeit in different ways. A couple of times each summer I will trim back the hedge around the stile. I think about the many walkers using this route, deliberately following each other's footsteps to avoid unnecessary damage to the meadow. Sometimes I will clamber into the roots of one of the ash trees and rest. In any event I will acknowledge them as the 'Grandmother' and 'Grandfather' trees. This is the place where a fallow deer was grazing on the other side of the hedge – I am not quite sure who was the more surprised by such a close encounter. On another occasion a hare tentatively made its way ever-closer towards me, before eventually picking up my scent and scoottling away.

The *land wights* made their presence too me quite unexpectedly by the ploughed-out barrows and I have acknowledged them there since. The barrows on the summit command at least a brief moment to honour the ancestors once interred beneath. This is my favourite place to watch the sun set, before heading home via other 'waymarks' I have not mentioned. I think of the whole walk as itself a ritual, with these various 'rites' taking place along the way.

While most people do not have a prehistoric landscape so close to home, allow places significant to you to become 'waymarks'. If you feel so inclined leave offerings which will degrade naturally. I am happier to mostly 'work on the inner' but that, in part, is because using visualisations has been a key part of what I do for many decades.

At the same time as you are consciously creating your waymarks, recognise yourself as the wayfarer. The way exists only in so much as there are both waymarks and wayfarers. The way creates both and is created by both. Creation creates itself.

## Life as a wayfarer

A specific journey is a 'waymark' of sorts in our overall life. We, as individuals, are like waymarks in the whole of creation. This is a 'way' we can never leave. It is always here, always now, always changing.

Such wayfaring is distinct from pilgrimage. The way is the destination. For traditional nomadic tribes life was places in walking distance put end-to-end. 'Walking distance' was as long as your life, no less and no more. The reality in the British Idles was probably more complex as waterbourne craft would have been at least as important as 'shanks pony'.

Events we deem significant act as waymarks along the path of life. These are generally referred to as 'rites of passage'. For what I hope are now self-evident reasons, it is as important to create – if only on our own – 'rituals' which add significance to what we regard as consequential happenings in our lives. Be prepared to help others 'invest' in such waymarks in their own lives.

## The *wyrmas* breath

The way of our life is the cosmos's way of manifesting its ever-emergent 'essence' or potency or gift. That 'essence' is the *leac* – or whatever word you prefer – I have already explored. Traditional myths and associated iconography depict this 'essence' as snakes and serpents.

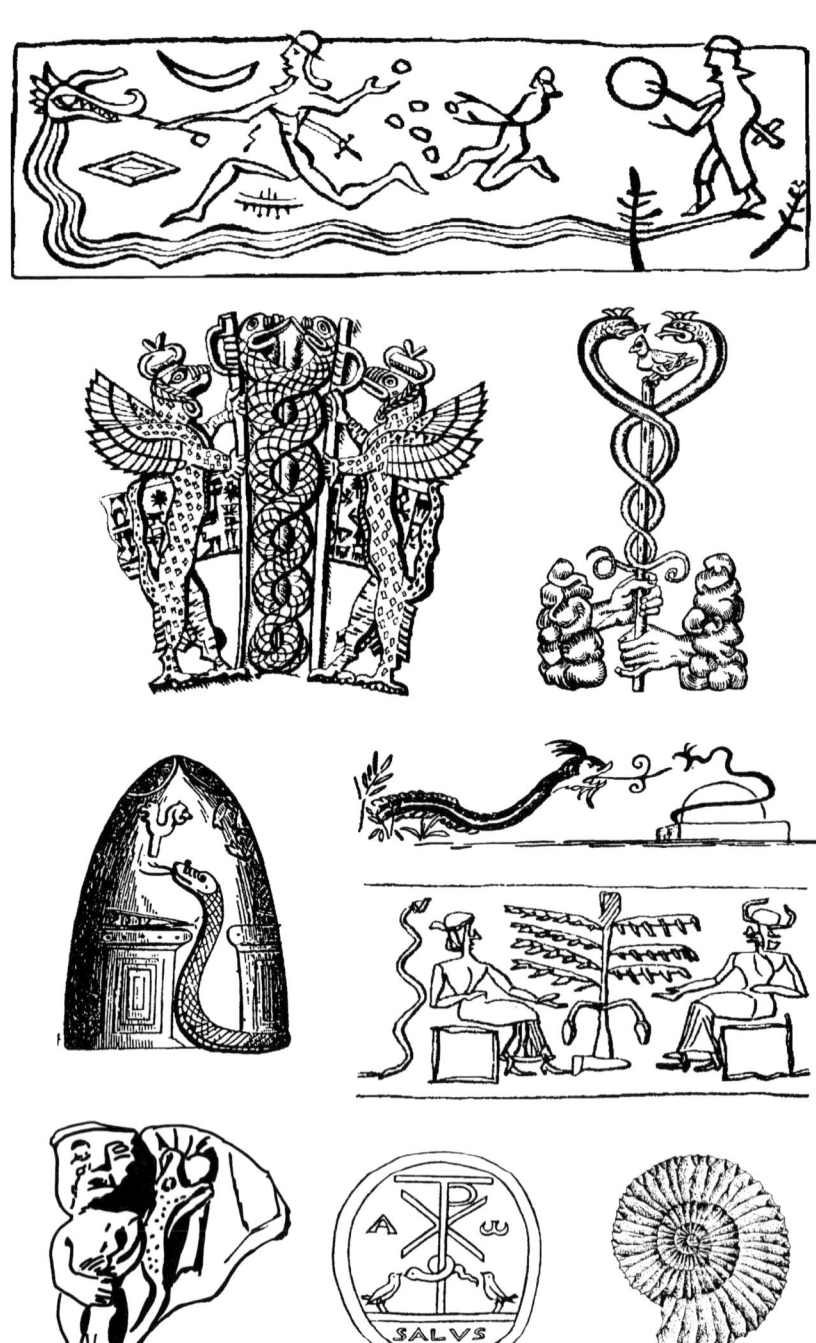

Only a brief moment's thought is needed to recognise why. Snakes are most often encountered when moving. Their peculiar manner of 'writhing' across an open surface of ground or water makes them appear to be the epitome of fluidity and ceaseless change. Furthermore, snakes shed their skins annually, allowing them to 'change form' in a unique manner.

Less often snakes are encountered when at rest, coiled up. They have, if I may play with words, 'potential energy' rather than manifest 'potency'. Their fluidity is, as it were, stored up. This is a perfect metaphor for a shrine – or other waymark on a pilgrimage route – where the power of the deity or spirit of place is concentrated. Think of a way and its waymarks as akin to writhing and resting snakes. This idea may not be intuitive to people in northern Europe who rarely encounter the indigenous species of snakes but, for me at least, it is a seductive one.

Snakes and their mythical kin, serpents, commonly occur in traditional lore and art. Christian thinking has introduced the sense of these as depictions of evil. But we must be careful not to project these back to pre-conversion thinking. Then snakes symbolised the power of medicines – and poisons. They were manifestations of the 'life spirit' of such concoctions. And bear in mind that distilled alcohols are commonly referred to as 'spirits' for this reason – the distillation process concentrated the spirit of wine. Once organic chemistry gained ground this 'spirit' was christened ethyl alcohol and, later, ethanol.

Opposite, from top:

*A serpents called Marduk features in the oldest-known legend, that of Gilgamesh.*

*Serpents continue to be prominent in Sumerian culture, evolving into the caduceus of Asclepius and then becoming a symbol for medicine.*

*A Babylonian 'omphalos stone (symbolising the navel of the world) protected by a snake. A wall painting in Pompleii depicts a serpent attacking a snake encircling an omphalos stone. The Tree of Life is associated with primoridial humans and a snake or serpent in numerous Middle Eastern legends.*

*One of those legends was recorded in the book of Geneesis and appears frequently in European art. Early depictions of the crucifixion have a snake rather than the body of Christ. We call them ammonites, but in British folklore they are 'snakestones'.*

*Avebury's twelfth century font with a bishop and two dragons – or are they wyrmas?*

Depictions of serpent-like beings known in Old English as *wyrmas* breathing out the 'life force' – discussed previously as *ond, óðr* and *leac* – straddled the conversion period. This iconography changed meaning around the twelfth century and became the fire-breathing dragons so familiar from later lore. But over-familiarity with this latter understanding of dragons should not blind us to the quite distinct meanings that similar-looking creatures had hitherto.

*The right-hand dragon or* wyrm *on the font.*

*This twelfth century tympanum at St Kenelm's church, Romsley, Worcestershire, shows Christ in Majesty flanked by two angels, with interlace* wyrmas *forming a vigorous border.*

The legend of Sigurd and the dragon is known from the thirteenth century Icelandic *Volsunga Saga*. But this tale was well-known long before as King Cnut commissioned a carving for one of the two minsters at Winchester. Sigurd's enemy transforms into a dragon to protect a hoard of gold. Sigurd slays his adversary. Thereupon Odin advises him to bathe in the blood there by obtaining invulnerability. Sigurd then drinks some of the blood, acquiring the language of the birds. This should be understood to mean that he now able to prophesise from the calls of birds. Finally, Sigurd roasts and eats the dragon's heart, giving him the wisdom of prophetic vision.

This I take to be something more than merely the ability to recognise portents and omens but more about be able to 'make them add up' as it were. All the powers Sigurd obtains from the dragon are exactly the sort of *leac* or 'charismatic gift' which seemingly fit with the early meanings of *wyrmas*.

I prefer the Old English words *wyrm* and *wyrmas* because they carry none of the baggage thrust upon words like 'serpent' or 'dragon'. Wyrmas, like serpents, can be sinuous and active or coiled and slumbering. There is much to be gained from recognising the ever-present interplay of these aspects. An overall sense of the *wyrm* as the 'way' is a powerful concept, more so when combined with sinuous and coiled manifestations of *wyrmas*, and further empowered by the concept of the *wyrmas leac* breathing in and out in an active/passive cycle.

# The babbling and bubbling meditation

Changing tack again, I want to take some of these conceptualisations into actual contemplative practice.

Living creatures, though mostly water, are what they are because of the parts that are 'earth', and because they breathe air. All animals are alive because of their ability to transmute oxygen into the energy which makes them alive. Not quite the same processes of oxidation which take place in a fire, but not that far removed.

All creatures, including you and me, are part of the ever-changing 'processes' of earth and fire, air and water. Learn to 'listen' to how each of these processes are different when experienced directly, as babbling streams, fires and wind – or by walking over the earth attentive to the geology and other processes which we so rarely think about. Then learn to recognise how those different processes reflect and manifest during your own different activities and moods.

Find a fairly remote place where you can watch a stream bubbling over rocks, where the water is alive and ever-changing. Briefly acknowledge and honour the *wights* of the place. Note how the energy is quite different to watching the flickering flames of a fire, or listening to strong wind blowing through the branches of trees in a wood. All these are 'alive' and ever-changing but in more dynamic ways than the earth. That too is ever-changing but on much slower timescales.

Spend as long at that place as you can without being disturbed. Allow your thoughts to merge with the babbling and bubbling of the water. Experience as best you can the *leac* of the water. Take away only your memories of the experience. Living water cannot be taken home in a bottle. Honour the *wights* again before leaving.

Begin to think about the way *wyrms* – or whatever name you prefer – so eloquently encompass so many key ideas of an ever-emergent cosmos manifesting as a way, whether active or passive at any one place or time, and with the 'potency' or *leac* breathing in and out as cycle. Once you have spent already spent some time 'thinking through' these multiple levels of meanings – and perhaps manifest some of these ideas as amulets or such like – then find a place which is a waymark – a 'shrine' if you prefer – on one of your ritual routes. Take the ideas, the amulets (or whatever) to this waymark and coil and

*Watery places can be so special that churches are built nearby. This is the eponymous spring-fed pool at Wells in Somerset.*

uncoil – mentally at least, literally as much as you can – these concepts and manifestations. 'Empower' the amulets with the *leac*.

If this reads as too generalised and woolly then apologies. I simply do not want to be over-prescriptive. You need to explore your own ways of where, when and how. You also need to have had previous experience of preparing for ritual activities as outlined in the previous books in this series. If you don't feel you are ready to take on this particular 'working' then perhaps you are indeed not yet ready…

## The ever-changing changeless tradition

Once we start looking for evidence of ever-emergent processes in societies then they start popping up, sometimes where least expected. In an almost self-referential way, one such manifestation is the way religions steady 'reinvent' themselves over the decades. One of the best examples are the many varieties of modern paganism. These have none of the overarching hierarchies of 'institutionalised' faiths so there is comparatively little 'inertia'. This corresponds to the considerable flux within the movement. There has been a new 'flavour' of paganism about every decade – although, predictably enough, new innovations are rarely to the taste of more established practitioners!

*Old illustrations of witches reveal much about the imaginations and prejudices of the artists. But little or nothing about what witches actually did.*

The beliefs and practices of modern pagans have little in common with what is regarded by some as indigenous European traditions of 'witchcraft'. Everything which can be said about this – including the choice of names to describe it – is deeply contentious. Quite a number of respected researchers have claimed this is purely of historic interest as there are no surviving practitioners. This belief entirely suits such practitioners as it means no one comes looking for them. The reality is that the people who are part of such a legacy are deeply secretive – even among themselves – and have no reasons to want people to know about them.

This begs the question as to how I know about them. Several are personal friends of mine – although I hasten to add that I do not count myself as one of them. What makes this a tradition is certain aptitudes and skills. What these people do, and the rationales they have for their practices, are entirely individual. And, contrary to superficial logic, this is what makes it a tradition.

Putting this the other way around, the most traditional forms of witchcraft are the most innovatory. This is because tradition has always been eclectic, always evaluating new ideas, taking those ideas and practices apart (so to speak) and putting back together the bits that really work. This tradition is rooted in ever-emergent practices, in which expediency overrules precedent.

Such emergence is the polar opposite to 'religions of the book', such as Judaism, Christianity and Islam. They each have canonical texts which ostensibly 'fossilise' the practices and beliefs. In reality these religions also evolve, both from 'bottom up' changes and 'top down' doctrinal mutations. Sometimes this leads to major schisms, as when the

*The text of the bible was mostly written in Hebrew, Greek and Aramaic before being translated into Latin. Subsequently it was translated into vernacular languages, such as English. Each time there have been subtle shifts of meaning.*

Orthodox and Latin churches went their separate ways, and again when Protestants rejected the Catholic church, or when Methodists split from the Church of England, and then split into three different ways of being a Methodist. Similarly, ever since the death of the Prophet Mohammed, there have been two distinct ways of being Moslem, Shi'a and Sunni, both of which have geographical variations. Similarly Jews can be Orthodox in several different ways, or members of various non-Orthodox movements.

In other words the claims that the canonical texts set out the one-and-only timeless way of worshipping Yahweh, Christ or Allah do not stand up to even moderately close inspection. The pace of change is slowed down in these 'top down' and hierarchical sects but nevertheless changes do come about. Anyone in Britain who has paid any attention to the protracted arguments within the Synod and laity of the Church of England will be aware just how painful the process is, whether acceptance of female priests (and, latterly, women bishops) or the acceptance of homosexuality among the clergy or congregation.

There are no such schisms and conflicts in traditional 'witchcraft', as it has been dubbed by others. Change and individual innovation are indistinguishable from the 'tradition' itself. Remember what I said earlier about folk lore and traditions as always dying out yet always being resurrected. What is deemed to be 'traditional witchcraft' is another fine example. It is a tradition which, from the bottom up, is a manifestation of an ever-emergent cosmos. And this – beyond any survivals of specific practices – is what makes the contrast with Christian worldviews.

# Ever-changing deities

If religions are best thought of as emergent, what about deities? Well only a moment's thought confirms that even within the most hidebound of faiths, the concepts of deity are ever-shifting. People seek out the deity or deities who fulfil an immense range of roles, often contradictory: an all-loving father figure, a martial smitter of enemies, a faultless mother, a bestower of mercy, the fount of all being, an all-knowing sage, a fun-loving trickster – the list is almost endless. Most seem like grotesque parodies of our fears and cravings. Devotion to omnipotent gods does seem, at least to me, little more than thinly-disguised fantasies of those whose hubris is so great as to crave being all-knowing, all-powerful alpha males.

It's as if people construct their notions of the divine from their conflicting desires. Indeed, are the first three words of the previous sentence needed? However you wish to answer that rhetorical remark, the overwhelming evidence is that concepts of the divine are ever-emergent. Not only the 'big gods and goddesses' but also the spirit-deities more commonly associated with day-to-day popular religion. I have referred several times to the *land wights*. As explained in *Knowing Your Guardians*, in Old English this referred to a wide range of beings, such as *aelfen, thyrs, eoten, dwearg, puca, scucca,* and *maere*. Some of these had characteristic forms – *thyrs* and *eoten* were giants, while *dwearg* were usually thought of as dwarves. But other entities were shape-shifters. By their very nature they were ever-emergent.

*Jupiter, the alpha male of the GReek pantheon, holding a staff and an eagle.*

*A reliquary in the shape of a shrine.*

Land wights evolve into the saints of early Christianity. The sheer number of early saints is mind-boggling as every early church seemingly was associated with at least one – although a small minority of saints were associated with more than one church. While the saints themselves did not mutate, the cult of their relics most certainly did. What constituted a relic began to encompass not just bodily parts but also cloth which had come into contact with them, or even the dust from their shrines. Smaller and smaller fragments of bones were – and still are – increasingly passed from church to church, greatly augmenting the available relics.

*The orishas ('deities') of Afro-American religions such as Candomblé, Obeah, Santería, Umbanda and Voudoun are similarly prolific, yet there are no limitations on new orishas being created by devotees.*

# The Orders or Choirs of Christian angels

First Sphere

- ❖ Seraphim
- ❖ Cherubim
- ❖ Thrones

Second Sphere

- ❖ Dominions or Lordships
- ❖ Virtues or Strongholds
- ❖ Powers or Authorities

Third Sphere

- ❖ Principalities or Rulers
- ❖ Archangels
- ❖ Angels

*The angelic choirs circling the abode of God, from Dante's* Paradiso, *illustrated by Gustave Doré.*

Interestingly, the highest order of angels – the Seraphim – are synonymous with serpents (although the literal translation is the 'burning ones').

Sometime around the fifth century an entire hierarchy of angelic beings was created, formalising the disparate descriptions in the Bible. In the New Testament, Jesus asks the name of the demon in a mad man, receiving the reply "I am Legion, for we are many.' Subsequently Christian ideologies have 'demonised' the deities of a great many other faiths, making any attempt to formalise the Christian understanding of demons a massive and ever-emergent task.

Surely, if the cosmos is in a state of continual creation, then the gods and 'spirits' are also part of this emergent process. After all, continual change is one of the main vital signs of all beings. Absence of such change is often regarded as evidence of death…

# Emergent self-identity

So, as you are presumably alive, you too are part of this emergent process? Or are you, like some deity defined in canonical texts, hidebound by your own past? Are you indeed unwittingly living in the shadow of an almighty He who created Aristotlean binary genders? Or have you begun to recognise it seems Ze created gender as an emergent process…

What society regards as normal for gender identity and sexual activity – 'cissexual' for short – risks becoming our children's sense of queer as gender fluidity takes over as normative. It's not that radical – David Bowie brought it to the fore of popular culture in the mid-1970s, except then the buzz word was 'androgynous'.

Not just gender, but all aspects of self-identity are in a 'state of emergency'. The magic – and I use the word quite intentionally – is to be aware of that emergent process we call 'self' and be willing to allow it to emerge and re-merge as the urges and needs arise.

We all change over time. Accidents and illness may lead to rapid change. Mostly we age slowly while changing our visible appearance several times a day by donning different clothes (and, less often, opting to wear none at all). Once we think of appearance as something which is more a matter of time than form then shape-shifting cease to be something associated only with the weirdest of paranormal beings. It is also the meta-metaphor of our own lives.

The belief that we have a single self seems to co-arise with belief in a monotheistic god. Both beliefs are entirely optional. I realise that some people have considerable difficulties with multiple personalities. Without wishing to trivialise the implications of such disorders, may I observe that a far greater number of people seem to have greater difficulties with 'singular' personalities. For me, the whole point about personalities – or personae as I tend to think of them – is that they must come with both an 'on' switch and an 'off' switch. While sometimes it can be difficult to find the former, we must always be sure about the latter.

# Identity fluidity

Personae with 'on' and 'off' switches. Surely this is stretching credulity beyond breaking point. Let me give you a few examples of how it works. I'll leave to a latter section how to develop a specific persona. In *Learning from the Ancestors* I've already used the metaphor of 'on' and 'off' switches when describing how rituals must have clearly defined beginnings and ends. Indeed within a ritual we almost naturally adopt a different persona. Sometimes only slightly different but there is a broad spectrum all the way to invoking deities (and I mean 'in-voking', not evoking which is merely calling them up). Any ritual which involves invoking even the most minor of deities needs a reliable and robust 'off switch'.

Living here at Avebury allows me to observe and, from time to time, engage with the modern pagans who arrive to take part in an assortment of rituals – usually the eight seasonal festivals but overlapping into handfastings and initiations. They are *visibly* pagan by their dress, jewellery, staffs, drums and so forth. No doubt some arrive without these 'trappings'. Undoubtedly some of the people who are obviously pagan dress in a similar manner most of the time. But I suspect most of them regard such visits as an opportunity to 'live out' a persona that is not the one that gets them through the workaday week. Avebury, for them, is akin to what in the 1980s became dubbed a TAZ – a 'temporary autonomous zone'.

Music festivals were the original TAZs, although these have become increasingly submerged in wider culture. Pagan camps remain excellent examples of TAZs, as presumably are many of the retreat centres of other paths. Rituals are, by their very nature, TAZs. Ritual TAZs need to be small and perfectly formed. They are ideal zones –

*Pagan ritual at Avebury, midwinter solstice 2012.*

spatially and temporally – for temporary personae when we can flip to a different way of being. Strictly it's more a different way of doing. Or, more exactly, a different way of 'emerging'.

While I cannot speak from personal experience, 'cos play' gatherings of fantasy fiction and scifi fans are clearly not a million miles different. Donning the costume is clearly the on switch, although without a clearer ritual 'context' I can only wonder about whether there are effective 'off switches'. There are clearly overlaps. But I think also the apparent distinctions are important.

There is another conspicuous overlap. In recent years the term 'lifestyle' as become imbued with some of the same sense of choice of how we prefer to live. The downside is that lifestyles are mostly usually adopted 'off the peg', as it were, from magazines promoting the interests of the vendors of the appropriate clothing and accessories – anything from the right brand of running shoes to the desired choice of car or postcode. My sense of personae shares the same sense of choosing options, but without the conspicuous consumption and insidious commercialisation. Rather than 'off the peg' the appropriate metaphor might be 'handcrafted'.

Rituals which mark rites of passage are explicitly about adopting new personae. Rites of adolescence are about the change from a child to a teenager. Celebrations of 'coming of age' are, in principle, about the transitions to being an adult. Engagements and weddings are about the shift from an individual persona to an identity as one part of a couple. Christenings both celebrate new life and act as a marker for the responsibilities and new 'ways of doing' associated with parenthood.

Divorce and bereavement are about 'uncoupling' personae and taking the first steps towards new social personae emerging in due course. Funerals are a more collective transformation, as in most cases many people need to 'uncouple' their personae from the deceased, or at least adopt a new type of 'relationship', one dominated by memories but often also coloured by strong emotions such as guilt or anger.

We do not normally think of the life cycle in terms of ever-emergent personae. This is perhaps a key weakness of the dominant model of individualism which has emerged in the last century or so. I simply find it easier to go through life – and all its various challenges and changes – with a more fluid sense of self, not least a recognition that 'self' often exists as just one part of a close relationship with partners, parents, siblings and so forth.

Allow me to share a specific example of this fluidity of identity. For about twenty-five years I had a succession of enjoyable and emotionally rewarding jobs. But none of my colleagues shared any of my non-work interests. And, by and large, I shared none of theirs! I became quite accustomed to having a smartly-dressed and ostensibly conventional 'nine-to-five' identity for as long as was needed, before 'flipping' to a much more casual way of living which was more in accord with my former existence as an art student with rather eclectic and decidedly 'alternative' interests. Quite self-consciously the donning of smart clothes most weekday mornings was a sense of 'putting on the motley'.

However, there was no such clearly defined 'off duty' persona. As I mixed with different groups of friends – spanning various fairly 'orthodox' community activities where I lived, various artist groups and assorted pagan meetings – different aspects of my personality naturally came to the fore. I felt little need to develop a specific persona for each, but nevertheless there was little overlap between these varied social activities.

All this happened quite naturally – as I am sure would be the case for most other people with broad interests. However I have come across people who find it difficult to 'compartmentalise' their lives and expect everyone else to be as interested their diverse pastimes as they are. Not necessarily a good way of keeping friends! 'Off' switches are important!

# Personae are more than pseudonyms

From the late 1980s onwards my leisure time pursuits increasingly involved writing. While this was dominated by what is deemed 'non-fiction', I quickly became aware that finding the right idiom for a particular readership was important. Most of my writing was done under my given name, although some of the idioms were distinctive enough that they could appear pseudonymously. This proved to be a good way to offer contrasting – although not contradictory – perspectives on a topic!

Some of these pseudonyms related to quite specific topics. But others were more open-ended. I discovered that they acquired 'personality traits' and looked at things in a different way to my 'default' persona. Initially this was an interesting 'exploration'. However I realised that it could work the other way. So, when I wanted to write a book in a different idiom to usual, I invented a persona and name which suited. This pseudonym was subsequently used for a few online articles, and surfaced as the fictional companion in another book which used Socratic dialogue in an unexpected context.

If you think this is verging on the bonkers then think again. This is exactly what every fiction writer does when 'getting into character'. Is writing a novel in which the first-person character is distinct from the author's own in some way fundamentally different from writing a non-fiction work though a pseuodnymous persona? Think of a novel in which the meta-narrative involves a heroine writing a non-fiction book, complete with some extensive drafts of that book-in-a-book. Now edit out the outer 'layer' so only the book-in-a-book is left? Get it? Well, you've got this book…

Writing itself can be regarded as a ritual. Indeed for many professional authors this is indeed the case as certain times of day, certain places, certain equipment become key to the process. As repeatedly noted, rituals are an ideal place to develop personae as they come with in built on and off switches. I can also 'turn on' one of these personae while walking around the Avebury landscape, seeing the world as it were anew through a fresh way of thinking.

If you want to make megabucks then don't refer to this as fiction or even non-fiction but call it 'channelling'. After all several million people seem happy to think that ancient Egyptian priests and Native

*The Neolithic Aveue from Avebury towards West Kennett, with beech tree clumps planted on Bronze Age burial mounds on the skyline.*

American tribal leaders – or whatever – speak perfect modern English in their afterlives. Far saner to accept that authors who create such 'characters' are evidence that the cosmos of capable of emerging in a wide variety of ways.

Envisage your 'individuality' neither as some over-specific sense of detachment, nor a 'pick and mix' from whichever exotic pasts appeal at the moment. Instead, see 'yourself' as a collection of identities which make up 'your selves'. Recognise that these identities have ancestors. Expand your sense of ancestorship to include significant teachers and role models – 'ancestors of tribe' if you like. So far as is practical, allow each of the identities to pursue their aspirations and 'have a life'.

These are the ancestors which I discussed how to honour and learn from in the second volume in this series, *Learning from the Ancestors*. When you get the opportunity reread this book in the light of the 'bigger picture' I have been presenting in this book. You should have a much richer sense of 'the ancestors' and how they are key to the concept of an ever-emerging cosmos.

# Investing in amulets

I have, for good reasons, allowed the section on using rituals as 'on' and 'off' switches to wander into some related topics. I promised some other examples of how to switch personae on and off. This next section assumes you have some experience of creating and reverting to personae within rituals. The next example requires that the creation process is inseparably linked to a physical object – perhaps an amulet or item of jewellery. For sake of convenience, in this example I will refer to it as a ring. Whatever it is, ideally you will have been made it – or, at the very least, done significantly modifications. There are exceptions, as when the item has been given to you by someone close or as part of one of their rites.

Put time and considerable effort into making the object and the associated persona. The aim is to have such a clear 'visualisation' of the persona and its associated mental 'attributes' that this can be called up more or less instantly by putting the ring on. The all-important 'off switch' is to take it off again. Clearly, unless the process of creation is tightly linked to the wearing of the ring then there is a risk that even after it is taken off the persona will persist. Think of it rather like a ghost – and deal with it accordingly.

There is a subtle variant of this which is useful for persona which are more confident, protective or – dare I say it – even downright aggressive. Such traits are not needed all the time but might be needed

*Amulets can be 'charged' with a full-on persona that you might need to call up in a moment of crisis*

in a hurry. Not the right time to be fumbling to put on a ring... Select something which you feel comfortable wearing all the time – it might be an item of jewellery, or something as unobtrusive as a fob for a key ring. 'Charge' it with a ful- on persona that you would need to call up in a crisis but would probably never want to 'act out' in other circumstances. When needed touch the object. At a pinch just visualise yourself holding it tightly in your fist. Practice finding the 'on switch' and shifting into this persona quickly. Martial arts training – getting into the mindset rather than the bodily postures – is relevant here.

One hint: such belligerent personae do not come with an easy-to-find off switch! Make sure you also create a relaxed, chilled out persona and 'attach' this to an entirely different amulet. Something made from wood or other natural materials is ideal. This persona is all about being a tree-hugging, blissed-out vegetarian. Maybe that's you on a normal day... In my case it's a persona I adopt as needed.

The commonest form of such 'instant access' amulets are the ones worn for luck – whether the traditional 'lucky rabbit's foot', or more specifically Christian ones such as St Christopher medallions, pilgrimage 'badges', crosses worn as pendants or such like. Pagans have plenty of counterparts to chose from, although they commonly wear them for other reasons than to bring them 'luck' when needed in a hurry. Strictly the word 'lucky' does not come from the Old English word *leac*, with all the connotations of potency. However 'lucky horseshoes' and other 'lucky charms' do seem to retaining this sense of some sort of inherent or 'channelled' power.

Amulets made from Milliput and pewter described in Knowing Your Guardians.

# Alternatives to amulets

Some people don't use a physical amulet at all to call up personae – they simply adopt specific hand gestures, or touch themselves in a specific way, such as tugging the left ear lobe with the right hand. If you have developed a 'routine' to ground yourself after meditating or doing a ritual then this is another example of how bodily actions can 'trigger' specific emotional changes. Priests do it differently – a variety of gestures are used as part of the liturgy. The Byzantine gesture of blessing

A friend of mine has a walking stick with eight different gemstones set just below where his fingers naturally fall. He can, as it were, 'dial up' a combination of characteristics. But this seems to me unnecessarily complicated.

I have no problem with personae with different dietary requirements. However I realise that friends and acquaintances may well regard major inconsistencies as problematic. We need to have 'default' settings when with family, work colleagues and among people we

A Byzantine-style tenth century carving of an angel at Breedon on the Hill, Leicestershire. The right hand is making a classic gesture of blessing. This same gesture is known as far away as Tibet where Buddhists today refer to it as lhasey zhon-nu.

*The top of a walking stick carved and owned by Bob Trubshaw.*

regularly share leisure-time pursuits. Those personae can be different from each other without causing problems. Many people are very different with work colleagues than when at home interacting with their children. We may even have specific personas that 'go with' individual friends, either because they share leisure interests or simply because this allows a more relaxed or even irreverent personae to come to the fore, perhaps at odds to the limits imposed by workaday expectations. There is, after all, nothing new about having a 'secret life' which transgresses the norms of the 'default' persona.

As Sandra Newman observed. 'the self might just be an agglomeration of masks, of all the roles we play, including the roles we play in private fantasies; a personal Mardi Gras that parades multifariously through our lives.'

Personae can – indeed should – be allowed to 'evolve' fairly steadily. Just make sure the other members of the social group are keeping up! If you're the sort of person who changes their dress and hairstyle quite radically on a regular basis then corresponding changes to personality will be much less of a surprise that if you always dress in a similar manner or fashion.

If personae created for protection or 'luck' / *leac* seemingly do the job then leave well alone. But if experience reveals that they need to be augmented or amended then there is no reason not to allow them to evolve. However in practice it is often hard to make one amulet or gesture call up the new concept rather than revert to the old one. The reality is that is often easier to start over. The exception would be when the amulet itself is at least as important as the persona it invokes.

There is no limit to how many such personae you need. However be sure that you are focusing on needs rather than desires. Allow little-used personae to step back – perhaps 'honouring' them from time to time as you would any other ancestors, but not calling upon them to do anything too pokey.

Indeed some personae – and their associated amulet – may be intended for one specific purpose. In which case, once their work is done, they *should* be allowed to 'retire'. In some cases a specific persona may cease to be helpful. In these exceptional cases the associated amulet may need to be burnt, buried, cast onto running water, or otherwise permanently 'decommissioned' and dematerialised.

# Playtime for personae

If all this sounds overly-serious then stop and remember the Eeenie Weenie. If an emergent cosmos is a playful one, then our transient selves and even more ephemeral sense of identity are part of the overall fun and games.

Personae need to have their chance to play as well as work. Make sure you have at least one persona who has a child-like love of running around, free from all cares, fond of larking about and telling jokes. Keep one or more serious ones too – but make sure the playful ones have a chance to take the mickey out of any self-importance that may arise.

Even more importantly, keep your sense of self-identity ever emergent. The needs for changes – and the rates of such changes – will be inherently variable. But getting 'stuck in a groove' for too long is not a healthy sign. This does not mean throwing everything overboard – just look for opportunities for one or more new personae to enter into your activities.

'Consistency,' opined Oscar Wilde, 'is the hobgoblin of small minds.' Peter Carroll had a greater idea:

> If you consider yourself an 'individual', in the sense of 'indivisible', you have not lived.
>
> If you merely consider yourself as a single being capable of playing various roles, then you have yet to play them *in extremis*.
>
> The selfs must allow each self a shot at its goal in life, if you wish to achieve any sense of fulfilment and remain sane.

# Creating personae

So far I have rather side-stepping both the nitty-gritty of creating personae and what sort of personae you might want to create. This is quite intentional – I want your own mind to come up with suitable scenarios before I begin to 'infect' your thinking with my own suggestions. Please stop for a moment and list the sort of personae that have popped into your mind, however vestigially, while reading the last few sections. Mostly these will seem like exaggerated versions of some of your wishes. That is just what they are. The needs for safety, wealth, health and fitness, understanding, power, companionship, fun and freedom, and so many others. We all have them. We often suppress the tendency for these understandable – but often conflicting and difficult to attain – desires to subtly dominate so many aspects of our thinking.

Call them out. Given them a name. Give them an appearance (anthropomorphic or otherwise). If you feel so inclined do drawings of them. 'Out' them in every sense. And give them the all-important off switch. By doing so you will take control back over your life. Except it will now seem like a multiplicity of lives. Some of these personae – the more aggressive ones – need to be given a clear place. There may indeed be times when you feel physically threatened and swap into such a personae. Hopefully most of the time you will not.

Some traits – such as the endless craving for more money – tend to gnaw away almost incessantly. Give it a name – Mammon is the most commonly used. Observe its many temples (though bear in mind most normal people call them 'shopping centres'). And use the off switch!

You are not me so I do not wish to tell you what sort of personae you might desire. Health, wealth and happiness are usually at the top of most people's wish lists. One or more 'protective' personae are handy for the more challenging moments that life may present us with. If there are any aspects of your work which you find especially demanding then you may wish to create a persona who 'maxes out' the desirable traits for that role – especially if those traits conflict with your more 'default' personae.

# Visualisation, ritualisation and actualisation

I have deliberately avoided discussing the creation of personae in guided visualisations (or whatever term you use). These visualisations arise within rituals and, if done properly, involve opening a 'doorway' of kind to get there, and closing it again on the way back. This is just another version of my on/off switch metaphor.

Normal dream states, waking dreams and day dreams should be regarded as distinct from such guided visualisations, if only because there is no clearly defined doorway or switch. If you are prone to 'going off on one' then I suggest you invest (mentally and otherwise) in an amulet which allows you to 'switch off'. If you already have a routine for grounding yourself after meditations or rituals that may suffice.

Above: *A stylised depiction of the* Deae Matronae.
Right: *A triple amulet inspired by this depiction.*

If you're new to this notion of inventing and developing personae but, instead, are comfortable with guided visualisations then I see no reason for using this as 'rehearsal space'. As neither of the qualifications in the previous sentence apply to me then I can't report from personal experience. The next step would be to 'meet' and adopt those personae within rituals. Once that feels comfortable then 'attach' a specific persona to a specific amulet (in the broadest sense – it may be jewellery or it may be a walking staff). Get used to having that amulet around without necessarily feeling the need to 'flip' into that persona, rather like you might get to know a new acquaintance who has quite a different take on life. When the time is right – and it may just happen 'by chance' – you can use the amulet to adopt the persona. Don't forget the off switch afterwards!

# That's why it's magic

The procedures I am describing – indeed insisting on are 'magic'. The magic allows you to switch personas at will rather than end up mired in personality disorders.

In a very real sense our desires become our beliefs. These desires and beliefs underpin the narratives which are core to our memories – and thus our sense of self identity. Memory and identity are two words for the same mental processes. People who lose their memory through brain injury are usually traumatised by their loss of self-identity. So, if you intentionally develop multiple identities, do not be surprised if you have more than one way of remembering past events. The past may not be completely mutable, but the meaning and significance we give to the past most certainly is. For this reason alone – and there are many more – self-identities are far more fun than monotheistic self-idnetity

All magic begins and ends with delusion. The initial illusion is that of consensus reality. The ultimate delusion is the reality of one's own magic. In between and along the way is where things are interesting.

The next book in the Living in the Magical World series is called *Enchantment is All About Us* and expands on these ideas, and offers many more.

# Acknowledgements

As with the previous books in this series my ideas have been inspired by a great many authors – who may be dismayed to see their ideas paraphrased without any reference to their own names. However in such a brief book then such 'niceties' must, regrettably, be omitted. Nevertheless, the relevant works are cited in the list of sources.

Among my personal friends I have been inspired most by Jamie Blackwater, Emma Restall Orr, Poppy Palin and Nigel Pennick. Insights and fundamental understandings have also come from many people who I know mostly or only through their writings or songs, including Peter J. Carroll, J.J. Clarke, Robert Cochrane, Lloyd D. Graham, Björk Guðmundsdóttir, Graham Harvey, Ronald Hutton, Tim Ingold, Michael Howard, Harold Roth and Daniel A. Schulke.

My thoughts on animism draw on much more extensive ideas by Graham Harvey, Tim Ingold and Emma Restall Orr. The remarks on reincarnation were inspired by listening to Kris Hughes' talk on death – as both a professional coroner and leader of a Druid order his perspective is nothing if not well-informed. Kris and Michelle Axe have both discussed *awen* with me, and the associated symbolism of the cauldron. Poppy Palin drew my attention to the poignancy of the rhyme 'Row, row, row your boat, gently down the stream'. The term 'Chaosmos' was invented by Peter J. Carroll; my own use of multiple personae developed after encountering Carroll's perspective about fifteen years ago. Writhing and resting snakes as a metaphor for ways and waymarks is taken from the writing of Daniel A. Schulke. My awareness of Robert Cochrane's legacy owes everything to the extensive work of the late Michael Howard, who overcome the many challenges this entailed and sent many insightful emails over the years.

The photographs on pages 9, 11, 12, 13, 15, 23, 25, 28, 37, 41, 46, 50, 53, 61, 64, 66, 68, 71 (right hand only) and the front cover were taken by Bob Trubshaw.

As ever, these acknowledgements would not be complete without acknowledging the inspiration and guidance of the *land wights* and ancestors of Avebury and north Leicestershire.

# Sources

Bey, Hakim, 1985, *T.A.Z.: The temporary autonomous zone, ontological anarchy, poetic terrorism*, Autonomedia; revised 1991.

BEY, Hakim, no date (mid-1990s), *Overcoming Tourism*; 1st publ. France; various English translations on Internet.

Carroll, Peter J., 1987, *Liber Null and Psychonaut*, Samuel Weiser 1987 (*Liber Null* first published 1978).

**Carroll, Peter J., 1995**, *PsyberMagick: Advanced ideas in Chaos Magick*; (2nd edn New Falcon 1997).

Chambers, Ian, 2009, 'St George: a Cainite myth?', *The Cauldron*, No.132, p3–5.

Clarke, J.J., 2000, *The Tao of the West: Western transformations of Taoist thought*, Routledge.

Cochrane, Robert, 2002, *The Robert Cochrane Letters: An insight into modern traditional witchcraft* (edited by Evan John Jones and Michael Howard), Capall Bann.

Danser, Simon, 2005, *The Myths of Reality*, Alternative Albion.

Graham, Lloyd D., 2010, 'Echoes of Antiquity in the Early Irish *Song of Amergin*', online at www.academia.edu/440504/Echoes_of_Antiquity_in_the_Early_Irish_Song_of_Amergin

Greywolf (Phillip Shalcrass), 1999, 'Awen: the Holy Spirit of Druidry'; online version at www.druidry.co.uk/what-is-druidry/awen-the-holy-spirit-of-druidry/

Harvey, Graham, 1997, *Listening People, Speaking Earth: Contemporary paganism*, Hurst.

Harvey, Graham, 2005, *Animism: Respecting the Living World*, Hurst.

Harvey, Graham, 2013, Food, Sex and Strangers: Understanding religion as everyday life, Acumen

Howard, Michael (ed), 2015, *The Roebuck in the Thicket: An anthology of the Robert Cochrane witchcraft tradition* (2nd ed), Capall Bann (1st edn 2001).

Hufford, David J., 1995, 'Beings without bodies: an experince-centered theory of the belief in spirits', in Barbara Walker (ed), *Out of the Ordinary: Folklore and the supernatural*, Utah State University Press.

', *Aeon* Hutton, Ronald, 2007, *The Druids*, Hambledon Continuum.

Hutton, Ronald, 2009, *Blood and Mistletoe: The history of the Druids in Britain,* Yale University Press.

Hutton, Ronald, 2013, *Pagan Britain*, Yale University Press.

Ingold, Tim, 2006, 'Rethinking the animate, re-animating thought', *Ethnos,* Vol 71:1, p9–20.

Ingold, Tim, 2007, 'Movement, knowledge and description', in D. Parkin and S. Ulijaszek (eds), *Holistic Anthropology: Emergence and conergence*, Berghahn Books.

Ingold, Tim, 2011, *Being Alive: Essays on movement, knowledge and description,* Routledge.

Ingold, Tim, 2013, 'Dreaming of dragons: on the imagination of real life', *Journal of the Royal Anthropological Institute.* Vol.19:4, p734–52.

Janowski, Monica, and Tim Ingold (eds), 2012, *Imagining Landscapes: Past, present and future*, Ashgate.

Johnston, Sarah Iles, 2008, *Ancient Greek Divination,* Wiley-Blackwell.

Kaliff, Anders, 2007, *Fire, Water, Heaven and Earth: Ritual practice and cosmology in ancient Scandinavia: an Indo-European perspective,* Riksantikvarieämbetet.

Klimo, Jon, 1987, *Channeling*, Tarcher. (Published in UK as *Psychics, Prophets and Mystics: Receiving information from paranormal sources*, Aquarian, 1991.)

Lakoff, George and Mark Johnson, 1999, *Philosophy in the Flesh: The embodied mind and its challenge to Western thought*, Basic Books.

Littlejohn, Ronnie, and Jeffrey Dippmann (eds), 2011, *Riding the Wind with Liezi: New perspectives on the Daoist classic,* State University of New York Press.

Morris, Brian, 2006, *Religion and Anthropology: A critical introduction*, Cambridge UP.

Newman, Sandra, 2015, 'Possessed by a mask', *Aeon*;  online at aeon.co/essays/how-masks-explain-the-psychology-behind-online-harassment

O'Connor, J. and J. Seymour, 1990, *Introducing Neuro-Linguistic Programming*, Crucible.

Orr, Emma Restall, 2012, *The Wakeful World: Animism, mind and the self in nature,* Moon Books.

Peek, Philip M., 1991, *African Divination Systems: Ways of knowing*, Indiana University Press.

Pennick, Nigel, 1995, *Secrets of East Anglian Magic*, Robert Hale.
Pennick, Nigel, 1988, *Games of the Gods: The origin of board games in magic and divination*, Rider.
Pennick, Nigel, 2006, *The Eldritch World*, Lear Books.
Pennick, Nigel, 2015, *Pagan Magic of the Northern Tradition*, Destiny.
Pollington, Stephen, 2000, *Leechcraft: Early English charms, plant-lore and healing*, Anglo-Saxon Books.
Pollington, Stephen, 2011, *The Elder Gods: The Otherworld of early England*, Anglo-Saxon Books.
Pollington, Stephen, Lindsay Kerr and Brett Hammond, 2010, *Wayland's Work: Anglo-Saxon art, myth and material culture 4th–7th century*, Anglo-Saxon Books.
Robertson, Stanley, 1988, *Exodus to Alford*, Balnain Books.
Robertson, Stanley, 2009, *Reek Roon a Camp Fire*, Birlinn.
Schulke, David A., 2006, 'Way and waymark: considerations of exilic wisdom in the Old Craft', *The Cauldron*, No.122, p3–5.
Stone, Alby, 1989, *Wyrd: Fate and destiny in northern European paganism*, published by author; 2nd edn Heart of Albion 1991.
Sudhir Kakar and Jeffrey J. Kripal (eds), 2012, *Seriously Strange: Thinking anew about psychical experiences*, Viking.
Thompson, Victoria, 2004, *Dying and Death in Later Anglo-Saxon England*, Boydell Press.
Trubshaw, Bob, 2003, *Explore Mythology*, Explore Books.
Trubshaw, Bob, 2005, *Sacred Places: Prehistory and popular imagination* Heart of Albion.
Trubshaw, Bob, 2007, *Horn Dance or Stag Night? Folklore and myth in the age of blogs*, Heart of Albion; online at www.hoap.co.uk/general.htm#HDSN
Trubshaw, Bob, 2012, *The Process of Reality: The curious continuity between early Chinese Taoism and early Greek philosophy*, Heart of Albion; online at www.hoap.co.uk/general.htm#tpor
Trubshaw Bob, 2013, *Souls, Spirits and Deities*,Heart of Albion (revised edn); online at www. hoap.co.uk/general.htm#ssd
Trubshaw, Bob, 2014, 'The queen of the valley'; online at www.indigogroup.co.uk/twilight/ast0340.htm
Trubshaw, Bob, 2015, 'The view from the henge bank: Henges – brands or performances?', *Northern Earth* No.141, p11–13.
Trubshaw, Bob, 2015, 'The view from the henge bank: All is change', *Northern Earth* No.143, p10–12.

Vásquez, Manuel A., 2011, *More Than Belief: A materialist theory of religion,* Oxford UP.
Walditch, Beatrice, 2014, *Listening to the Stones,* Heart of Albion.
Walditch, Beatrice, 2015, *Knowing Your Guardians,* Heart of Albion.
Walditch, Beatrice, 2015, *Learning from the Ancestors,* Heart of Albion.
Watts, Alan, 1962, *The Joyous Cosmology,* Vintage Books.
Weir, Anthony, no date, translation of *An Cailleach Bhéara* (*The Lament of the Old Woman of Beare*), online at www.beyond-the-pale.co.uk/lament.htm
Yanying Lu, 2012, 'Water metaphors in Dao de jing: a conceptual analysis, *Open Journal of Modern Linguistics,* Vol.2, No.4, 151–8; online at www.scirp.org/journal/PaperDownload.aspx?paperID=25478

*Also from Heart of Albion*

# Listening to the Stones

**Beatrice Walditch**

*Listening to the Stones* teaches you to 'listen' – with all your senses – to revered places. Beatrice Walditch uses the prehistoric henge and stone circles at Avebury as her main examples, but wants you to explore and 'listen' to sacred sites near to where you live.

This is the first book in the Living in a Magical World series. These books will challenge you to recognise the traditional magic still alive in modern society, and empower you with a variety of skills and insights.

ISBN 978-1-905646-26-5  2014, 215 x 138 mm , 84 + vi pages, 49 b&w photos, 9 line drawings; paperback. **£9.95**

*Also from Heart of Albion*

# Knowing Your Guardians

## Beatrice Walditch

*Knowing Your Guardians* provides advice and inspiration to help understand the various ways of thinking about protective guardians. Beatrice Walditch mostly explores the traditional 'spirits of place' in Britain, although also shows how similar ideas and concepts are found elsewhere in Europe and beyond. She shows how these guardians have long been thought to have a 'potency' or 'luck'. The final sections of the book explain how to make amulets and 'charge' them so that they act as personal guardians.

This is the second book in the Living in a Magical World series.

ISBN 978-1-905646-30-1 2015. Demi 8vo (215 x 138 mm), 86 + vi pages, 57 b&w photos, 15 line drawings, paperback. **£9.95**

*Also from Heart of Albion*

# Learning from the Ancestors

## Beatrice Walditch

In almost every traditional culture throughout the world, including Europe until comparatively recent times, there have been ways of 'honouring' at least some of the dead, those who were regarded as key founders and ancestors. Learning from the Ancestors shows how such traditional ways of thinking – and doing – are of benefit in the modern Western world.

Beatrice Walditch mostly explores the ancestors of England, although also shows how similar ideas and concepts are found elsewhere in Britain and beyond. She explains how 'listening' and learning from the ancestors should be done in a ritual manner, not necessarily in ways which would be appropriate in other situations.

*Learning from the Ancestors* is the third book in the Living in a Magical World series. These books will challenge you to recognise the traditional magic still alive in modern society, and empower you with a variety of skills and insights.

ISBN 978-1-905646-27-2. 2015. 215 x 138 mm , 72 + viii pages, 28 b&w photos, 5 line drawings; paperback.
**£9.95**

*Also from Heart of Albion*

# You Don't Just Drink It!

## What you need to know – and do – before drinking mead

**Beatrice Walditch**

**Illustrated by David Taylor**

Mead is the oldest-known alcoholic drink and familiar to a great many traditional societies throughout the world. For Druids it is the appropriate ritual offering to the ancestors. In medieval legends it is the source of poetic inspiration. In the British Isles mead-making may go back as far as five thousand years ago, to the time of the prehistoric henges.

Every bottle of mead is part of this unbroken tradition. So, as Beatrice Walditch explains, *You Don't Just Drink It!* In this informative yet light-hearted book she tells you what you need to know – and do – before drinking mead. She also includes recipes and practical advice for brewing mead, based on her own experience.

Above all, *You Don't Just Drink It!* reveals why sharing a bottle of mead with friends needs to be done at the full moon…

ISBN 978-1-905646-24-1  2012. Demi 8vo (215 x 138 mm), 73 + iv pages, 18 b&w photos, 4 line drawings, plus vignettes, paperback. **£9.95**

# Heart of Albion

Publishing folklore, mythology and local history since 1989

Further details of all Heart of Albion titles online at
**www.hoap.co.uk**

All titles available direct from Heart of Albion.
Please add £1.30 p&p (UK only; email
**albion@indigogroup.co.uk** for overseas postage).

To order books please contact

**Heart of Albion**
113 High Street, Avebury
Marlborough, SN8 1RF

Phone: 01672 539077

email: albion@indigogroup.co.uk
Web site: www.hoap.co.uk